THE GIFT OF AUTISM

A Journey of Joy

Rebekah J. Shumway

A Mother's account of the first few years following her daughter's diagnosis of autism disorder, and the joyful discoveries hidden in the journey that is life.

Rebekah J. Shumway

The Gift of Autism; 2010 Rebekah J. Shumway.

All rights reserved.

Copyright ©2010 Rebekah J. Shumway

ISBN 978-0-557-39806-5

FOR

Spencer, Sydney, Isaac, Samuel, Anna
and Brian;
Who is my favorite person of all.

Rebekah J. Shumway

TABLE OF CONTENTS

Introduction	7
Setting The Stage	9
First Signs	17
Diagnostic Shock	27
Gift 1: From Mourning To Morning	35
Gift 2: God's Tender Mercies	56
Tender Mercy #1—Our Community Of Support	57
Tender Mercy #2—Toys!	64
Tender Mercy #3—Statistics 100	68
Tender Mercy #4—A Tight Budget	72
Tender Mercy #5—Hurray For Siblings	80
Gift 3: Learning To Love	91
Learning To Love Brian	91
Learning To Show Affection	95
Learning To Laugh	101
Pearls Of Love	106
Pearls From School	107
Pearls Of Empathy	124
Learning To Let Go	127
Gift 4: The Joy Of Discovery	134
Gift 5: A Life's Education	144
Gift 6: Celebrating Our Uniqueness	155
Conclusion	164
Acknowledgements	171

Rebekah J. Shumway

Introduction

Early in the spring of 2004 our world was turned upside down when one of our children was diagnosed with autism disorder. It would be impossible to describe all the feelings and events that followed, but I want to share a little bit of the journey that our family has taken. Our daughter's autism has changed every aspect of our lives. I am certain it has played a role in shaping who her brothers are now, and how they will perceive the world around them as they grow. As parents, her autism has changed us in hundreds of ways.

When we received her diagnosis it felt as though our world had ended. Our daughter was alive and well, but our hopes and expectations for her future were shattered. To us it was like a death. Now that we are several years into this experience, the adventure has turned into something totally different. Her diagnosis was just the beginning of our understanding new expectations and acquiring new dreams. We had no idea what wonderful things were waiting for us.

This isn't a book about curing autism. Despite all that has been written about autism, from a medical perspective there is still no cure for autism. While substantial progress has been made developing therapeutic interventions in recent years, autism is a neurological disorder for which there is no silver bullet. In the past, expert opinion was that an autism diagnosis essentially closed the door on social and cognitive development. That is not true anymore. As early intervention strategies are increasingly used, children with autism are not only developing more normally than ever before, but are also ascending heights previously considered impossible.

This isn't a book about defining autism, although a little of that is probably necessary for those readers who are not on this journey themselves. This is a book about my daughter's autism—which is different from any other autism in the world. Sydney's autism is unique, and every person with autism has their own story and their own struggles and victories. Specifically, this is a book about the very early years of autism: those years between finding a diagnosis and finding peace and joy.

This is a book about discovery. There is a lot in this book about the discoveries we made that helped our daughter. I hope to inspire someone to investigate some of the things we've done, perhaps to discover a treasure of hope for their loved one: but, that is not the primary purpose of this book.

This book is about growth. Life doesn't always go as planned for many reasons. Autism is just one bump in the road that a family can experience. Bumps like autism look like Mt. Everest when you are wallowing in the mud at the base of them, but those bumps also provide views that are hard to come by without the elevation change. Our "autism view" has enhanced our lives substantially. Choices we make and experiences we have shape us. This book is as much about the way our family changed as a result of our daughter's autism, as it is about how she has grown. Mostly this book is about the joy that we have found, not in spite of her autism, but as a direct result of it.

This is a book about discovering the divinity in trials and finding the joy in living life as it is handed to you. This book is a story—a story of a mommy, a daddy, some brothers, and a sister in the middle. This book is the story of a special gift that was given to a child—but not just to the child, to her entire family. This book is a story about receiving the gift of autism.

Setting the Stage

I grew up in a home with parents who were very realistic about life. I went into marriage and then motherhood with my eyes wide open—knowing that I was in for a lot of hard work and sacrifice. However, I was not prepared for how it would be, *really*. I wasn't prepared to love so deeply and completely that my soul would ache for a way to express it. I wasn't prepared for the agony a parent suffers just in anticipation of what might possibly go wrong. I wasn't prepared to be totally enraptured—a complete captive of the moods, accomplishments and personality of the little person named Spencer who first came into our home.

After Spencer arrived, I worked at home as an engineer. I went to great lengths to not work while he was awake. Otherwise, as he sat at my feet beside my computer, I was drawn to turn from my work and look into his sparkly blue eyes and listen to him coo. My husband and I both knew we had the smartest baby in the whole world. Every new expression was captivating, and every new sound an attempted word. We were hopelessly smitten. I was completely guilt-ridden over the time I spent away from him—short as it may have been.

Spencer was still an infant when we decided we wanted him to have a sibling. Soon I was expecting again, and our afternoons together consisted of me sprawled on the couch with him crawling around on the floor beside me. One afternoon I was trying desperately to get a nap while he tried just as hard to get me up to play. In exasperation, I pulled him onto my chest and squeezed him close, "Spencer, I love you!" He sat up on me and took my face between his soft, squishy hands, "Ahh mos, ahh mos, ah mos." I laughed right out loud, "It sounds like you want me to say I love you the most!" He squealed and burrowed his head into the side of my neck. I was delighted at his successful communication, and thrilled that he wanted my undivided love. At the same time, anxiety welled up within me—how would this new baby fit into our little family? How would I love a new child? Was it possible to love that much again? How would Spencer feel once he was no longer the center of my universe? Was it fair for him to have to share my attention and affection so soon?

My first and second pregnancies were very different. The first time, I wanted to shout the news from the rooftops! It took all my self-control to wait until the 12-week ultrasound before I announced it at work. My husband and I decided we would wait for a while before telling anyone, but that lasted about 24 hours—I simply had to tell my mother, my brothers and sisters, my close friends at work and church. The second time around, I felt protective of our news. I didn't want anyone to say the wrong thing about it and cheapen the miracle, the blessing, and the wonder of it. I hoped to avoid the questions about whether or not it was "planned" or a "mistake." My introspective feelings were enhanced by family events. Two thousand miles away my mother's death was looming after a long struggle with ovarian cancer. The life I carried inside me was so comforting—as though I had a secret shield to fight off the dark and gloom. I hurt a close friend because I had not confided in her the good news until I was over six months pregnant—but I couldn't explain to her that my pregnancy, this baby, was my protection from deep, deep sadness; I feared others would not understand how special it was.

Spencer had buoyed up our confidence as parents. Baby number two? Sure, no problem! In addition to his responsive and playful disposition, he was also very rational. When Spencer was three weeks old he was crying inconsolably in the middle of the night.

Finally, out of desperation, I said out loud, "If you are going to cry if I hold you, then I am going to put you down!" He immediately stopped crying. I was so surprised, I poked at my husband until his groggy eyes opened and I could recount the experience to him. Another reasonable, low maintenance, brilliant, darling little boy—that was what I thought I wanted.

Boys' names had been easy, we had lists of boys' names we liked written out in hundreds of different permutations up and down pages in a spiral notebook. Girls' names were harder. Brian didn't like what I liked, and vice-versa. I really didn't like the name he liked the most: Sydney. The Olympics were held in Sydney, Australia that year, and I teased him that it was a dumb thing after which to name a child. Several weeks before my delivery I had a dream. In the dream I saw a smiling, darling little girl with dark pigtails whose name was Sydney Kay—named after my mother, Shelly Kay. From that moment on my baby was Sydney Kay and she was mine.

Sydney was perfect—perfectly round, perfectly pink, perfectly soft and perfectly loved by her 17-month-old brother. We have a video recording of Spencer meeting Sydney for the first time. My grandmotherly nurse at the hospital saw Spencer, and asked if big brother would like to pick up his sister from the nursery. He went with his daddy, they scrubbed up, and Brian held him over her bassinet. He leaned away from Brian to get down close enough to kiss her. The nurse then let him "push" her bassinet down the hallway to my room, and he laughed the entire way. Once in our room, Sydney continued to be the center of his attention. He sat with me on the bed, kissing her head, pulling off her hat and exploring her entire little person. It was obvious that this was a special big brother. Our first night at home Spencer wouldn't leave my side as I fed the baby. He didn't want to go to bed. I sensed that he didn't want to leave us. So I said, "Spencer, Sydney will be here in the morning when you wake up. We get to keep her. She is ours." He laughed and clapped his hands, slipped off the couch and went upstairs with his daddy.

We called our families—Sydney is here, a blond little pink thing! My mother and father were on the line, "Honey, that is wonderful," "We are so glad." My heart ached with loneliness. I knew that they were too consumed by what was looming ahead to really feel joy over my little baby.

That night I accidentally pulled off Sydney's stocking cap trying to arrange her in her blanket. The cap shrunk off behind her head and revealed a smock of down-soft dark-brown hair. Brown hair! For a good twelve hours I had thought that my new baby had blonde hair! The next morning I made the calls again, correcting the very important detail. My family thought it was very funny that I would miss a simple detail like her hair color. I was so glad she had dark hair! It made her even more like my mother, my precious mother who was slipping through our arms and into the world from which my daughter had just come.

When Sydney was two weeks old my mother's condition worsened dramatically. We changed our plane tickets to come home earlier than we had planned so my mother could see her before she died. I put Sydney in one crib and Spencer in another and let them cry for what seemed an eternity while I threw clothes and toiletries into a suitcase. I called a friend at work and asked if she could fly home with me. She left her husband a note, and Brian drove us to the airport.

I flew into Salt Lake City with my two babies late that night and went to the care center where they had moved my mother to die. She was asleep, so we went home to put my exhausted children to bed. I spent that night in my parents' room, listening to the sounds in the house, feeling disturbed by the unfamiliar hospice smells brought by my mother's illness and watching my daughter sleep in the car seat by the bed. So much had changed, the sight of my daughter felt like the most familiar thing in the room. My sister came in; we stayed awake all night, too full of feelings to sleep.

The next morning I went with my new baby to the care center and sat with my mother and her friend Laurel while my father went home and showered. My mother slept beside us while I visited with her friend and held my baby. When my dad came back, the nurse came in and checked my mother. He said to my dad, "She is not changing. Normally that can mean she is waiting for someone to tell her it's okay to die." The nurse left and my dad said, "We have told her it is okay to die. She is waiting to hold Sydney."

Laurel picked up my tiny daughter and laid her on my mother's chest. She held my mother's hand to my baby's head and said, "Tell her about your baby, Becky."

I leaned over her cancer-ravaged frame, looked into her sleeping face and said, "Mommy, this is my baby. We named her after you. We named her Sydney Kay. She is a beautiful little girl. She has dark hair just like you. She is soft and beautiful, and I wanted you to see her…" I talked and cried until it was more than I could take. I turned and my father held me while I sobbed. I took my baby daughter and my toddler son, and went home to my parents' house, a house that now reeked of absence. That evening, my mother died.

Sydney was my special gift. She was my reminder that life goes on in spite of death. She was joy and peace in the days that followed that are still surreal in my memory, as we prepared for the funeral and burial of my mother. The distraction of my children was a wonderful blessing; they prevented the heaviness from settling in too deep. The night of the viewing I had been in the reception line for about 30 minutes before my aunt came and found me and announced that she "needed" Sydney for a while. I watched her walk away with my perfect sleeping baby pressed up against her lips, and watched the pain settle from my aunt's eyes a little. I knew exactly how she felt.

The Sunday after we buried my mother we blessed our Sydney in my father's ward. My entire family, and a large showing from my husband's family, gathered in the Relief Society room with my father's bishop in a brief meeting before church. My husband, our brothers, our fathers, and a few close friends stood in a circle with little Sydney in the middle and blessed our little angel, welcoming her to earth and giving her a name.

In Sydney's blessing, Brian blessed her to be a "special friend to your mother." At the time, Brian was aware that I had a fear of teenage girls. I remembered the hard time my sisters and I gave my parents as teenagers and adolescents—I was afraid of being on the receiving end of that heartache. I was grateful that he would think to include in her blessing that we could be friends. Later, that blessing took on new meaning for me.

Sydney was a fussy baby; she did not like to be put down, so I obliged. I slept propped up on pillows with her sleeping on my chest. I held her for hours sitting on the couch. I cried and snuggled her and talked on the phone to my sisters. I didn't mind that she needed to be held so much, in fact I didn't even notice. She was my security blanket, my comfort. My mother was dead, and Sydney was my gift from God, my compensation for that loss. Looking back, I was terribly depressed. I chose to treat that depression with high-doses of chocolate. Chocolate ice cream, chocolate chip cookies, candy bars, brownies—I wasn't choosy. One day I realized that it had been two days since I had eaten something that wasn't chocolate. I was even hiding the wrappers from the chocolate—tucking them under the dirty diapers in the garbage to hide them from my husband. Two days into a chocolate fast I called my sister and told her that I was in bad shape. She said, "Oh that's nothing, I just fed my two-year-old Doritos and ice cream for breakfast! At least it is only your health you are wrecking."

My children were such a blessing during that difficult time. Caring for them was therapeutic and distracting. One day, several weeks after my mother's death, my husband and I were playing with the kids when something they did made us laugh. I don't even remember what happened, but I do remember how it felt. It felt so good to laugh again. They were a large part of my healing, and a reminder that life goes on—joy in life can endure through heartache.

For the first year of Sydney's life we lived in the married student housing at The Ohio State University where we grew close to a particular neighbor. Our friend, Merry, was an employee of Franklin County. She worked with parents and teachers writing Individualized Education Plan (IEP) goals for kids with developmental disabilities in Columbus Public Schools. Merry had heart-wrenching stories of her "special" kids and their families. One day we were out at the chain link fence along the road behind our apartments, letting Spencer chase the cars up and down the street safely behind the fence. Sydney played in the grass at our feet and we had a long conversation about kids and Merry's work. I asked, "Would it be harder or easier for you to have a special needs child now, knowing what you do about special education?" She told me it would be harder, because she would know what she was in for from the beginning. I told her, "I think I could handle just about any handicap except autism—that would be the worst for me."

Sydney, our autistic little Sydney, sat right there at our feet. I had just announced that autism was a trial I didn't want and didn't think I could handle, and God already had it in store for me. God had given me a child with autism, and He would give me the tools I would need to prove myself wrong—I *could* handle it.

First Signs

Having a baby is one of my favorite things to do. There is something magical and almost surreal about the hours and days that follow the moment that you hold your baby in your arms for the very first time. I'm not talking about the nasty hospital smell, the constant stream of intruders, the exhaustion, the medicated fog, or the terrible hospital bed; I'm talking about those moments when it is just you, your baby, and the angels from Heaven. It's those times when you are in total awe at this brand new life, the moments you can't count the toes, stroke the soft head, or kiss the silky cheeks enough. It's those moments when you think this baby is in some way still a part of you—and you are completely humbled by this perfect little person and the Creator that gave him or her life.

The afternoon after Sydney was born I was having just such a moment. A young girl with a hospital neck badge came into my room and told me she was there to test Sydney's hearing. She asked me to sign the papers and then to let her take Sydney for a few minutes. I let the young girl wheel her bassinet into the hallway, totally unconcerned. It took an unusually long time for her to bring her back. When she did, she told me that Sydney failed her hearing screening, and that they went ahead and did an ABR (Auditory Brainstem Response) test too—which she also failed. She told me we needed to schedule another hearing test at Children's Hospital. The news left me feeling very upset and a little numb.

Upon my arrival home, my first order of business was to call Children's and schedule the second ABR hearing test. The test would be six weeks away! It seemed like an eternity to wait and see if something was wrong. I started reading about deafness and succeeded in scaring myself silly over it. At Sydney's two week check-up I told my doctor what had happened, she told me not to worry, she had seen lots of kids flunk the screening and come out fine in the end. She told me, "I can tell by the way that baby is responding that she hears just fine."

I took a hungry, tired, sleep-deprived Sydney to the hospital the day of her test. The audiologist attached some sensors to Sydney's little head and neck and then let me nurse her to sleep. The test results came back totally normal. Sydney's brain was hearing sound just fine. I was so relieved. My anxiety was just a sampling of the anxiety that can consume a parent who thinks something might be wrong—or who knows something isn't right.

Sydney was three months old before she slept lying down by herself. She had severe acid reflux complete with projectile vomiting. Our pediatrician recommended giving her Maalox every four hours or so. Sydney hated the taste of it, and always blew as much as she could out of her mouth. For months I always had white drops of dried Maalox on my clothes, on the walls, and all over her. Maalox seemed to help immensely, but it didn't solve her sleeping problems. We attributed both her insomnia and her fussiness to acid reflux, well past the six months of age at which babies are supposed to outgrow it.

Sydney was shy, even coy. She wouldn't look at us or play with us like Spencer did. One night Brian pulled her from the bathtub and was trying to play with her. He called me to come into the room. "Watch this Becky." He put his face right in front of her, and called gently, "Sydney," she turned her head to avoid him. He called again, "Sydney," and moved his face to be in her line of vision. Again she turned her face away. He said, "She will not look at me! She is my coy little girl!" I noticed that she was not avoiding his gaze in a playful manner, her little face was expressionless as she moved her eyes away from his. I knew my husband had been painfully shy as a child; his mother told stories of sitting in the hallway outside his Sunday school class so he could peek out the door to be certain she was still there. I wondered how early shyness starts, and how it manifests itself? Brian and I mentioned offhand to each other that we thought it was a little strange.

She was slow doing everything—sitting up, crawling, eating solids, and walking. At the time I said, "Sydney is not sitting yet, but I don't mind having a baby a while longer." And I meant it. I was delighted by her smallness, her babyness. I was determined not to be the hyper-worried mom who fretted over every little milestone that wasn't reached exactly when other kids were doing it.

At Sydney's two-month check up I mentioned to the doctor that she wasn't smiling at us. The doctor told me not to worry—it was a little early for that anyhow. At four months I repeated the concern, and the doctor reassured me that babies come with their own personalities. By six months we were saying to other people, "Sydney is so different from her brother, she is shy. They come as their own people, don't they?" Around eight months old, she laughed for the first time. She laughed at Spencer. A friend asked me about when she first smiled, and I didn't know. As a baby, she never smiled in the same way that other children do. She only smiled when *something* was funny to her—never because she enjoyed *someone*.

Sydney was a very sensitive baby. My sister gave me a baby swing when Sydney was born. It was a wonderful little portable swing that had a panel of lights above the baby's head with music that played when you turned it on or when the baby hit at the toys that hung from the top. Spencer loved it. He squealed when we turned it on and quickly learned how to turn it on himself. To Sydney, the swing was a torture device. When Sydney was in the swing, she acted terrified of the lights and hanging toys. If Spencer turned it on, she trembled and went stiff, and started to hyperventilate—a classic "fight or flight" response to this silly toy. I thought at the time it was strange that they would design a toy for a newborn that was so terrifying. Later on, we hypothesized that it was terrifying to Sydney because she was so oversensitive to things. Sounds, sights, smell, the way things feel—these things are informative to you and me. To her, and many other individuals with autism, they can be intrusive and frightening.

We left Ohio for a residency in Texas when Spencer was not quite three and Sydney was 16 months old. Up until we moved, Sydney's aloof behavior and her slow development did not worry us at all. We laughed about the funny things she did, and I loved feeling like we still had a "baby" in Sydney—long after most kids don't have much baby left in them. Sometimes I wish we had known earlier, so we could have started her therapy sooner. At the same time, I am grateful that I enjoyed Sydney's first 18 months—free of the fretting, heartache, and burden that her diagnosis brought. We enjoyed aspects of Sydney that we thought were uniquely hers.

Our apartment swimming pool in Texas was perfect for our little family. It had a shallow area with fountains that led into the larger pool, and most of the time we were the only people at the pool. We went during the day in the summer heat, and then went back in the evening as the sun was setting. Spencer and Sydney loved the water, and Spencer moved from toy to toy and from one water activity to another. He easily made up elaborate games and loved to be pulled through the water by Mom or Dad. Sydney had one activity at the pool. She stood by the side of the pool in the shallow section and dipped her hands into the water at her feet, and then patted them in the puddle on the side. Over and over, this was the game she played at the pool. We pulled her away to show her the fountain, and she went right back to the wall. We pulled her into the deeper pool and held her to our chests, and she became tense and frightened and wanted back at the wall. She didn't want cups or watering cans or balls or floaties or ducks or any of the other toys we brought—just the wall and the water at her feet. We thought it was cute, funny behavior, and we videotaped it.

Brian and I started wondering if her behavior was "normal." We had concerns about her lack of attention to us, her lack of smiling, and her repetitive behaviors. A big concern for us was her sleeping—or rather, her total lack of sleeping. She took hours and hours going to sleep at night. She was often awake well past midnight. It was also not unusual for her to awaken in the middle of the night and be awake for the rest of the night. Sometimes when she was awake she was almost manically happy--kicking and singing, babbling louder and louder. But sometimes she was very distraught--screaming and crying, impossible to console, and impossible to put back to sleep. Even before we moved to Texas, she never slept in a crib because we found that she preferred the portable playpen, and we liked being able to move it out of the nursery and downstairs into the living room in the middle of the night. Sometimes the only way to get any sleep at all was to move her into a room as far from the rest of the family as possible and let her scream herself to sleep.

The first time we let her "scream it out" she was eight months old. After four hours of screaming, I went and picked her up and then held her through another two hours of screaming until finally she passed out. Food, a new diaper, burping, baby Tylenol, a drive in the car, a walk outside, new pajamas—we tried everything and nothing seemed to help. Once we were in Texas, it was harder to escape the noise of her nighttime activities. It was not uncommon for us to strap her into a car seat and put her in front of a video at 2 a.m. Eventually she was going to sleep in the car seat and staying in the car seat most nights, all night. I thought it was reflux and that sleeping propped up would help.

Brian and I did discuss the possibility that our Sydney had autism. We knew enough about autism to recognize that some of her peculiarities were similar to autism traits, but she was so darling! I never really believed that she was actually autistic.

We had a close friend who was a resident at the VA hospital with my husband. She was around us a lot after work and on weekends. One night after dinner, with Sydney humming to herself and running circles in the family room, she nonchalantly commented, "Look at Sydney in her own little world." She then called her name several times, "Sydney, Sydney." After receiving no response, she said, "I wonder if she could have autism?"

Hearing our friend suggest that Sydney had autism raised some "mamma bear" red flags. It's one thing for a parent to be hyper-worried that something is wrong; it's another thing if others start to notice. I decided I would talk to my pediatrician about the possibility of autism at Sydney's 18-month check-up.

When the day of the check-up arrived, I talked myself out of being concerned about autism. That day, we waited for two hours for our name to be called, the office staff treated us poorly, and I was flustered from trying to entertain my children in a crowded waiting room.

Once in the examining room things just got worse. I couldn't believe the things my active three year old was finding wedged in the cracks of the examining table and around it on the floor. About the time I had to pull hypodermic needle caps off Spencer's fingers, I decided any concerns I had could wait until another day. I would not raise them with the doctor on *this* day.

The doctor finally breezed in, took a quick look at Sydney and asked three or four developmental questions that I answered very briefly. She then told me that Sydney might be autistic. She wanted to refer her to some specialists for an evaluation, and directed me to have her hearing checked. She was with us for all of about four minutes. This made me very angry. Brian and I could talk about autism and it didn't upset me—but to have a pediatrician suggest that she had autism after such a short evaluation made me mad.

I left, intending to never return and to find another pediatrician. The doctor made the referral, and I received a packet in the mail from the developmental pediatrician with pages and pages of questions to answer regarding Sydney's development. I tucked them into the stack of papers on my counter and told myself that I would wait to fill them out—let's give her some time to "grow out of it." After all, these doctors did not know my little girl like I did.

I did go ahead and get her hearing checked, again. I had no idea what it would be like, and I took Sydney's three-year-old brother along. We had to go into a little sound booth for the test, and Spencer couldn't come. I explained to him that he had to sit on a chair in the hallway next to the technician, and that he wouldn't be able to see us or hear us, but he couldn't get off the chair or make noise. He sat there for 45 minutes without moving or peeping.

I read in several books that the siblings of special needs kids are often little adults—they grow up much earlier than their peers. They assume responsibility and seem to have a sense of when to "cut Mom and Dad a break." This has been the case with Spencer. His good behavior that day made up for his sisters'. She was terrified in the little sound booth and would not cooperate. The talking puppets, the far-off noises—she clawed at my neck and tried climbing up onto my head to try to get away from it. The technician had to technically fail her, but she told me she was able to discern that in at least one ear Sydney could hear well enough to learn to talk. Brian and I suspected her hearing was good, because she loved music and came running when we played the piano or sang. But she certainly acted deaf when it came to acknowledging or understanding what we said and in trying to talk herself.

Over the next few months Sydney did make progress. We caught occasional glimmers of normalcy—times when she was really enjoying an activity with her brother. She discovered books. One in particular, *Brown Bear, Brown Bear*, she could even recite to herself, even though she had no useful or purposeful language at all. We saw her make many improvements, but noticed other things that started to unravel.

Sydney became very unhappy. We had days when she screamed for as much as seven hours in a 12-hour day, followed by screaming most of the night. She was almost impossible to take anywhere—especially other people's homes and church. I chalked it up to her "shyness" and teething, but I was being pushed to my limits emotionally and physically. I found myself getting angry with her when she was upset, and I was frightened by my feelings. I was getting sharp with the kids and short-tempered.

One day in particular stands out in my memory as an illustration of what was going on in our lives. Sydney was in an insomnia cycle and I was up with her most of the night, and then at about 5:00 a.m. she started crying non-stop. It was almost 11:00 a.m. when my visiting teachers stopped by to see us. I had completely forgotten that they were coming. None of us were dressed, and dishes, crusted with the mostly untouched breakfast remnants, were still on the table. Toys were strewn everywhere in the front room, and in a desperate attempt at happiness I allowed Spencer to play in some packaging peanuts and he had spread them all over the apartment.

My friends came in and sat down and I sat and tried to visit with them with Sydney clawing at me, screaming at me in my lap. I started to cry too, and I couldn't stop. I apologized, and at seven months pregnant, I told them I was just having "pregnancy hormone" problems. Without a word, one of my friends stood up and took Sydney from me and disappeared into the bedroom. In a few minutes, Sydney was asleep, and my friend put her in her crib. She came back out, and I continued to cry. They told me they were going to run some errands, and could Spencer come too? They hauled him off to Wal-Mart without shoes, in his pajamas, and left me to cry for another 45 minutes. Not long after that, I got serious about filling out the paperwork for her evaluation. "Even if she does not have autism, maybe they can help us with her sleeping problems!" I reasoned.

Filling out the pages of paperwork was upsetting and eye-opening. For many of the questions, it was obvious what the answer was *supposed to be* for a neuro-typical child. The more questions I answered, the more I knew that the responses I had to provide painted Sydney into a category that was not neuro-typical. I felt there were still holes in the profile I was creating about Sydney. I typed up a separate document, cataloging the recent progress and personalizing the profile. I mailed the information back to the clinic. Not long afterwards I got a call from the clinic. They felt that Sydney did need an evaluation, and they had an opening in a month from a cancellation. They were also sending more paperwork, more evaluations to fill out. It had been four months since the initial pediatrician's visit and my referral had expired, and I had changed pediatricians. I made an appointment with my new pediatrician to renew the referral. At that visit, the pediatrician was not as hurried and asked a lot of questions. Her response was the same as the first pediatrician, "You need to have this little girl evaluated for autism."

In my mind I was still playing a game with the medical professionals. They didn't know Sydney like I did. They could be totally wrong. "These people are just being cautious with us," I reasoned. I was in denial. February 17th loomed in front of me and I couldn't wait to get there and get it over with.

Diagnostic Shock

The weeks preceding February 17th I grew increasingly anxious that something was wrong. The evaluations I filled out brought my attention to other peculiar behaviors Sydney had. As I met with playgroups and friends, I was more aware of her isolation from other children and her "strangeness." I grew frustrated with friends who were ignorant about autism. When I mentioned to several that we were having the evaluation done, they said, "There is nothing wrong with Sydney! Look at her! She is so cute." And then in the same breath they said, "She's in her own little world, isn't she?" They were unaware that the "cuteness" of little Sydney, her humming, her ballerina-walking, her distance from others, her repetitive play, were all manifestations of a neurological disorder that could stifle our baby's learning and her future.

As Brian left for work the day of the evaluation, I said, "Remember, this is for informational purposes only. We can disregard anything they say." He smiled at me, kissed me and left without answering. A friend watched Spencer that afternoon, and I met my husband at the hospital. I was tense and nervous, and I got lost in the hospital complex. I was looking for the San Antonio Children's Hospital Village of Hope, but I didn't want to ask anyone for directions. I was acting as though I were ashamed. I didn't want anyone thinking that something could be wrong with the little girl in my arms.

The Village of Hope is a cluster of buildings on the end of the Hospital property that was converted into offices and a diagnostic clinic. I met my husband and we were ushered into a room filled with people. Introductions began: developmental pediatrician, neurologist, two speech therapists, two occupational therapists, a physical therapist, a social worker, and a parent liaison. They started the evaluation, playing with Sydney and taking turns asking questions to further clarify the information from our previous correspondence. They had obviously read her file carefully. I was impressed with how well they knew Sydney, and how they interacted with her.

Coming into the appointment, I was certain she wouldn't cooperate—that it would be a repeat of our audiologist experience. I was surprised at how well they related to her. They were kind and complimentary; every little response was met with enthusiastic praise, and real excitement about what she *could* do. I felt myself begin to trust this group of people and to love them for the way they handled Sydney. Both Brian and I felt she was herself, what they saw in the evaluation was what we saw at home. Sydney sat in a little desk in front of us, surrounded by strangers, in a very stressful environment and acted exactly like herself, as though that was what her life was like every day. I said a silent prayer of gratitude in my heart. I wanted an accurate diagnosis. I knew the team needed to see what we saw to get it right. I had not believed it was possible.

At the end of the evaluation the team left and discussed Sydney's case for about 30 minutes. When they came back inside, they talked to us about their conclusions. The developmental pediatrician knelt on the floor in front of us to talk to us. She showed us charts where they had mapped Sydney's developmental levels in different areas. She was seriously delayed in her communication and social skills. In fact, in her communication skills, she was still at newborn level, 0-3 months old, in spite of being one month shy of her second birthday. The communication delay made it hard to tell what her cognitive level was, and she had milder delays in her gross motor skills.

THE GIFT OF AUTISM

The developmental pediatrician explained very carefully the criteria for autism as specified in the DSM IV (Diagnostic Statistics Manual, edition four), and then told us that Sydney had "mild to moderate autism disorder." She then said, "I hate to say this to any parent, especially a parent who is nine months pregnant, but the chances of you having another child with an autism disorder are one in four." She was gentle and careful, and seemed as nervous as I felt. I reached down and pulled Sydney into my lap. I wanted to tuck her away—hide her from these people now. Suddenly they were the bad guys, and I felt an emotional fence go up.

Sydney struggled to get down, and I hesitated to let her go, but did so to avoid a scene. I was embarrassed at my reaction. I started to dab at my eyes and sniffle; I bit my cheek—hard. Brian's first question was "What is the long-term prognosis?" The team talked in vague terms about the successful therapies that were out there now, and the many resources… The pediatrician said, "I even saw a book recently about the marriage relationships of autistic individuals," and then to others in the room rather than us, "Who would've thought that individuals with autism would marry?"

The comment was casual; she meant it as encouraging. But we only knew a few symptoms of autism in children; we had no idea of the long-term implications, we hadn't even thought them through before. Instead of encouraging, her words came like a slap in the face. Sydney wouldn't marry? That had never occurred to me. Instantly, Sydney's diagnosis seemed very grim. Would she ever talk to us? Would she ever learn to read? Would she ever hold a job? Would she ever love us? Who was this little girl? The doctor was saying something else, "While Sydney can improve drastically and make wonderful progress, she will probably always have some residual autism."

Residual autism…residual, residue…something left over…like particles of food that don't get rinsed off in the dishwasher and end up glued inside the glasses. Or maybe like my neighbor who had polio as a child and had a slight limp—or at least I was told she limped, I never noticed it. "Residual autism" gave me hope—perhaps autism was something we could put in our past. We could recover from autism and only be left with a little social "limp." Or maybe "residual autism" was like breaking your neck and having "residual" paralysis. My moment of hope was squashed by a torrent of panic.

Our time was up; another child was coming in for an evaluation. We were led into a foyer area to a round table with two people seated at the table. Who were these people again? My head was swimming. I had to ask them twice. One was a social worker, the other a parent liaison, "What is a parent liaison?" I wondered.

I was shocked at her diagnosis, and I was surprised at my shock. We said the "A" word for months previously, knowing it might be so, but it was so painful to be told that she *was autistic*. Tears started to roll down my cheeks and I held my breath to keep from making noise. I couldn't stop the constant flow.

I cried all the way through the meeting with the "social worker" that followed. I wanted to say very curtly, *"We don't need a social worker!"* Social workers are for people with family pathology and major problems. *"There is no problem here!"* I wanted to scream. I couldn't look at the people across the table from me, my husband talked to them about the brochures they handed him. My eyes were fixed on Sydney.   She was tilting her head back and forth and humming as she danced on her toes around an imaginary circle on the floor next to the table where we sat. My little Sydney, my sweet baby, what was in store for you now?

We finally got up from the table, and I practically ran for the door. Once outside, I started to sob audibly. Brian wrapped me into his arms and held me while I cried right there on the sidewalk. Sydney strained to get down, not seeming to notice our grief. A very apprehensive employee approached us; would we please come back in to sign some paperwork and take a picture? I pushed away from Brian, embarrassed that we were not alone. I didn't just push him away physically; I started to push him away emotionally too. I was angry, and he would get the brunt of that anger for the next terrible while. I wrote a check out to "The Village of Hope" for the co-pay to our visit. I was struck by the irony of the name. I felt no hope. Instead, I felt like my world turned upside down and my dreams for my little girl were pounded into a billion bits.

Relationships have a natural give and take—a rhythm to them. Before Sydney's autism, I never thought about it. I never would have realized that we treated Sydney any differently from her older brother if she hadn't been diagnosed with autism. Ten minutes after her diagnosis I realized that we were doing things that exacerbated her exile from us, and I recognized that we needed help to know how to reach our baby girl and help her grow. From the time Spencer was a newborn, I talked to him while we were in the car. I talked to him to soothe him when he fussed, sang to him and pointed to things as we drove. Once I was alone in the car with Sydney, I realized that we didn't talk to her like we did her brother. She never responded to us, so we had largely stopped talking to her. We drove in silence, my heart breaking and tears dripping off the end of my nose. I tried a few times to comment to her about what we were seeing, and each time I looked in the rearview mirror—desperate to see her respond, to prove to everyone that she was fine—and each time I cried harder as she hummed to herself and looked around as though she were the only person in the car.

We picked up Spencer and went home. It took me hours before I could call my dad and tell him. It was the next day before I called my in-laws. I refused to open the door and refused to answer the phone. Finally, after two days and a dozen phone messages from my sister, I answered one of her calls. I couldn't look at Sydney without crying. I didn't want anyone to know—I wanted to protect her, keep it a secret. I had never felt so dead.

I called my little sister, Emily, and tearfully reported the doctor's diagnosis. Instead of responding in surprise, she said, "I have known something was wrong with Sydney from the day you blessed her. Brian blessed her that she would be your special friend, and I thought that probably meant that she would never leave you."

I was startled and upset about this wrinkle in my perfect denial. The doctors were wrong! How could my sister think such a thing? Later, I was comforted to know that God had whispered to my sister that her niece was special. Since then, I like to think that Sydney being my "special friend" means that we will forge a bond, as a result of our years of labor together, learning.

A few days later, I was at a friend's house for lunch. It was a playgroup that we held weekly for months. But this time when we went, everything was different with me. I told my friend that Sydney had been diagnosed with autism. I started to cry. My friend started to argue with me. "Nothing is wrong with Sydney, how did they get that diagnosis? Are you going for a second opinion? That has to be wrong."

Our voices grew louder, and the kids left to play in the backyard, everyone except Sydney. She stayed in the kitchen and played with the blinds as though nothing was wrong. I argued with my friend, she voiced all the things I felt, and I countered her arguments with my limited autism knowledge and the traits Sydney had that fit the diagnosis. The tables had turned on me. My friend was angry, frightened for me and in denial. My new role was to convince my friend that yes, there was something very wrong with Sydney. I cried and cried as we argued, but it was a very important exercise for me in overcoming my denial. My friend was upset because she loved Sydney. I loved her for loving my little girl. That friend once told me that she loved best those people who loved her children. Her "fight" with me that day over Sydney's diagnosis endeared her to me.

One reason an autism diagnosis is hard is because it is so life altering and is often not detected until the child is older. There is no blood test, and there are usually no accompanying dysmorphic physical features that would alert a doctor to the problem when the baby is born. Parents can be tormented wondering "What did we do wrong? What caused this? What changed our baby?" It is easy to feel that some event changed your baby; although in our case Sydney had always been different, but it became increasingly apparent as she grew older.

The good news is; autism detection is improving drastically. When Sydney was diagnosed, the pediatrician told us that most of her patients were between 3-5 years old, but her goal was to get to the point where all of her referral patients were 18 months old. Two years later, I received a brochure for a conference to discuss the detection of autism in infants as young as five months old. This progress is so encouraging. Early detection means early intervention that leads to better end results, and early detection means fewer compounding variables that muddle evidence that can unlock the mystery of what causes autism. Unfortunately, until that happens, parents of kids with autism are in for a real shock. You have a perfect baby, you have a perception of this baby, and then that perception is turned upside down when your toddler's peers start exhibiting their personalities and curiosity, and your toddler still acts like a newborn. One evening after the older children were in bed, we were sitting on the couch, and Brian was holding our tiny new Isaac in his arms. After a few minutes of silence, Brian whispered to our sleeping infant, "Oh Isaac, if you are autistic too, it would break my soul."

A family must go through a real grieving process when a child is diagnosed with a disability or disease. The only experience I had to compare it to was my mother's death. Sydney wasn't dead, but my perception of her had died. My dreams for her had died. Our plans had been turned upside down, and we had to start over with a new Sydney, our Sydney with autism.

Gift 1: From Mourning to Morning

During this period, I read in a book that someday you will look at your child and only see the child and not the disorder. I ached for that to be true. I felt as though a monster came in, kidnapped my girl and left someone else in her place. She had not changed, but we had. Now, everything that had been difficult about Sydney before became heart wrenching.

Every minute she was awake at night I laid awake too, listening to her sounds through the wall between our beds. I was horrified that she wasn't sleeping; horrified that this was one of the elements of autism. I worried that she was too tired to learn the next day and that with every minute she was awake at night we were falling farther and farther behind in her development.

Her screaming that started out of the blue, sometimes in the middle of the night, and could continue for hours, used to be extremely frustrating and exhausting. Now it was terrifying. What was going on inside her? Was she hurting? What was happening to our girl? Her refusal to acknowledge us used to just strike me as shyness and "different from her brother." Now it was like a personal rejection: I was reminded every time I called her name or tried to speak to her that she had autism disorder.

I felt like we were not only robbed of our dreams for her future, but we were robbed of the happy memories we had of her as a baby too. It was shattering when we discovered that some of her cute ways were really manifestations of autism disorder.

For example, Sydney hated being on her stomach so much, she didn't ever soldier crawl. Instead, she waved her legs back and forth in front of her while sitting, rocked back and forth, and scooted around on her bottom. At the time, we thought it was cute; we probably own 30 minutes of camcorder footage of her scooting on her bottom! Later, after she was diagnosed with autism, we had a goal with the physical therapist to get Sydney comfortable being in prone position. The therapist pointed out that Sydney was never on her stomach—even going down stairs or sliding off a chair or couch. Suddenly what was cute when she was a baby was something that needed therapy to fix. This was heartbreaking to us.

Our one connection with Sydney was through music. We could get her attention by singing much more successfully than any other way. In fact, most all of her non-screaming vocalizations were either while she was "reading" books or while she was singing. She hummed and ran in circles and we thought. "Oh how cute!" She recited her favorite book and we thought, "Oh how clever!" Then we learned that the humming, the running in circles, and the memorizing favorite books—were all very common activities of kids with autism.

Anytime someone you love is diagnosed with something, you find out that people who know someone else in your situation surround you. This can be helpful, but it can also be frustrating.

One friend from church called to talk to me about her cousin with autism. She asked me if Sydney engaged in "hand flapping." I thought, "Oh that sounds weird." And then I confidently told her, "No, we have never seen that." Not long after that, we watched a special on TV about autism, and horrified, I watched a group of young kids behaving exactly like my daughter. When excited, they bounced or jumped up and down, with arms bent at the elbows, hands "flapping," just exactly like Sydney. I had never even noticed it before. Brian said, "Becky, those kids act just like Sydney." I didn't answer him.

The day after her diagnosis at the Village of Hope, the developmental pediatrician called to check on us. I was embarrassed; I must have been quite a scene—hysterical pregnant lady with unfortunate husband and autistic daughter. She was kind and encouraging. She told me about a lecture she was giving on autism to a group of doctors in the area, would we like to attend? She encouraged me to look at the recommended reading list she included in the packet of information the social worker gave us. I hadn't even opened it. Her phone call brought me out of my shock and helped me determine to do something about Sydney's autism. It cemented my resolve to become an autism expert. I would cure my daughter. I would know everything about autism. Deep down, I hoped that the more I read, the more concretely I could prove that they were wrong, Sydney didn't really have autism disorder. We found the opposite to be true.

My first autism book purchase was at a Half-Price bookstore in San Antonio. My husband and I read it out loud together in the hospital while I was in labor with Isaac, one week after Sydney's diagnosis. I was frustrated with Brian that he was not as focused on the reading as I was. He was distracted. Looking back I can laugh at myself, of course he was distracted, we were having a baby!

The more I read the more terrified and desperate I became. Daily I added behaviors to my list of things that were cute in Sydney before that were sickening to me now. Sydney's personality seemed to disappear from me. Previously, I didn't know what autism was. As I read, many things that I thought were Sydney were actually elements of her autism. I felt as though autism ate up my daughter, right in front of my eyes. In reality, she wasn't changing, I was.

Rebekah J. Shumway

Included in some of my early reading were others' personal experiences with autism. These left me feeling angry and frightened. One day my father called, and found me hysterical from my reading. He told me I could not read anything of a subjective nature and I should stick to the scientific literature. He could see that the case reports I had been studying had too much emotional information, and were paralyzing my ability and desire to act. I took his advice, and that helped me for a long time. In the beginning I needed unemotional information so I could see clearly to make rational decisions.

For the most part, this autism-reading binge was like dumping lemon juice on a paper-cut. The more I read, the more the autism diagnosis fit, and therefore the more it hurt. I felt totally paralyzed. It took several weeks to get up the courage to start making the phone calls they recommended—the first one was to a group that provided training to parents of children with autism, called "Any Baby Can." The second call was to Easter Seals in San Antonio. It would be several weeks before an evaluation could be done, and then rotations with therapists would be arranged. This was an agonizing wait. I was reading like I was cramming for an exam, but it was desperate reading—I wanted to find out how to "fix" the problems with our little girl. Everything I read emphasized early and intensive intervention, but I had no idea what that meant. What were we supposed to do? By now I knew a fair amount about autism disorder. I knew enough to know that we did have it, enough to be really frightened by it, but not enough to know what to do about it.

Previously, when we lived in Ohio, there was a fad among some of the young families with whom we associated to teach their babies sign language. At the time, I thought it was a very silly thing to do. In my mind, it ranked up there with insisting that your child learns to read at four, and was a manifestation of hyper-driven parenthood. "Good grief, just wait until they can talk!" I thought to myself.

Sydney's first speech therapist recommended that we start teaching Sydney sign language. This was my first helping of autism humble pie. I was so angry about the whole thing—and totally overwhelmed. Teach her to sign? Did that mean they were telling me she would never talk? Why would a child who has perfectly normal hearing need to use sign language? I admit I dragged my feet—for about a week. Before long, desperation set in, and teaching Sydney to sign became my number one priority. After all, I had to *do* something. The problem was, I wasn't sure how to go about it. Where do I start? I was paralyzed by my own fear. Looking back, it is so ironic to me that those first steps were so hard. Doing therapy with a special needs child is not rocket science. I have a degree in chemical engineering, my husband is a dentist, surely we could figure this out—but it was totally overwhelming to me.

I knew a few signs in American Sign Language: "more," "I love you," and the alphabet—all from watching *Sesame Street* as a child. I also knew a few church primary songs with actions—was that sign language? Certainly the words "commandment," and "Savior" in sign language are important to know... I decided that "more" was the only really helpful thing I knew.

I was in the kitchen eating some raisins when Sydney wandered in and started looking around. She didn't point at what I was eating, she didn't fuss for something to eat; she just stood there, looking at my hands that held the raisins. I knew she was hungry. I knew she would love a raisin. I decided to give the sign language thing a try, following the description of some therapy I read about in a book. I said, "Do you want a raisin?" She just stood there. I knelt down in front of her and I gave her a raisin. I said, "Do you want more?" and I signed "more." Then I took her hands in mine, helped her sign "more" and gave her a raisin. I repeated this over and over. We ate raisins together one at a time while my mind raced and I summoned up the courage to be disappointed. I said, "Do you want more?" I signed "more," but I didn't take her hands and do it for her—I waited. She paused for a moment, and then her little hands came together, fingers kissing. "Hurray!" I yelled. I gave her a handful of raisins. It was the first time my daughter had ever "told" me anything. It was the first time she realized that she could do something to communicate what she wanted. Looking back, she was just learning to imitate, she had no idea what the sign for "more" meant, but imitation is a very important step on the road to communication. I started to believe that we could do something about her autism—we *could* reach into her little world.

My raisin success was like a gun firing—shooting me out of the starting blocks (even though the trick would not be repeated later for her Father). I knew I needed more signs than just "more." I looked online at the library catalog; I couldn't find a book that just taught simple signs. Somehow dragging my three-year-old, my autistic and unhappy two-year-old, and my two-week-old to the library sounded like more than I could handle. I called the parent liaison from the Village of Hope—I seemed to remember that her son used sign language. She told me to use a web site called firstsigns.org. This ended up being a website on the *first signs that a child has autism*, not the *first signs a child with autism should learn*. I tried searching on the Internet...my super-slow dial-up connection would not let me view the video examples of how to do signs.

After several days of frustrating dead-ends, I remembered, my sister knows sign language! I called her immediately. "Cathy, I have to teach Sydney to sign, I need your help!" Her reply, "I have a package ready to mail to you; I was just waiting for you to ask." I was surprised, "Why would you wait until I asked?" Her reply was a little hesitant, "Well, you told me you didn't want people telling you what to do." She was absolutely right. I said that to her. I called her one night, hysterical, and told her that I was tired of getting unsolicited advice from people who know nothing about autism on what to do with my daughter.

Catherine served as a missionary in southern California. For her last area, her mission president decided to place her in the ASL mission. He put her with a deaf companion and had her work in the deaf community. This meant a serious crash course in American Sign Language. At the time, Catherine wondered about the transfer so close to the end of her mission. Her mission president told her, "I have a feeling you will need this skill later in your life." Catherine's mission president was right for a lot of reasons, and her first opportunity came within her own family.

Sydney loved books. Catherine described over the phone how to make the sign that meant "read a book" by tracing the finger of one hand across the palm of your other hand, like you were tracing the words in a book. Sydney picked up on this sign almost immediately, and for a good while she used "read a book" to sign for anything she wanted. Catherine sent the package, including manuals and videos. Some friends from Ohio sent me a video series made for hearing children to learn very basic sign language; a former mission companion sent me an ASL dictionary. We were on our way to teaching Sydney how to communicate.

Spencer loved the signing videos. Sydney liked them too, but she didn't understand them like her brother did. Initially, I used the videos as a babysitter. I turned on the signing video and then disappeared to do laundry, put on deodorant, or brush my teeth, whatever. Soon, Spencer knew more sign language than I did. I consulted him if I was uncertain about something. I also made more than one phone call to my sister along the lines of, "Please tell me how to sign watermelon!" We discovered the key to getting Sydney to communicate was to find those things that really motivated her and exploit them.

In the beginning, she often resisted when we tried to take her hands in ours to make the signs. She also ignored us unless we were tempting her with something very enticing. It was hard at first, but in several months she had four or five signs: more, read-a-book, bubble, swing, and cookie. Soon, she was even saying the words as she signed them. Sydney wasn't non-verbal anymore. Sign language taught her about communication, and for the first time she understood that the sounds we make have meaning—so I thought.

For everything, we still had to "show" her what to say in order for her to know what to do. She didn't initiate requests. Very often we had to help her sign by taking her hands in ours and making the sign. Sometimes, she just held out her hands, wanting us to help her sign whatever it was she wanted.

Then one day, I was sitting on the couch and she wandered over and leaned into my lap. She looked down at her tiny hands, signed "cookie" and said, "cookie." It took a moment for me to understand what she was doing. I couldn't believe my eyes. I think I frightened her; I jumped up from the couch so quickly, flew into the kitchen with her and gave her an Oreo cookie. I called my speech therapist and told her. She said, "Did you dump the entire bag of cookies into her lap? Next time she does that, give her the entire bag!"

Sydney's signing was going so well, but that didn't mean that we didn't have setbacks. Sydney "babbled" in sign. She walked around the house humming and making all the signs that we taught her. My initial excitement at her communication was squelched as I realized that she was just practicing moving her fingers in the ways we had shown her.

I thought Sydney didn't really understand the meaning of the words or signs she used. It seemed she had just learned to echo what we prompted her to say in order to get what she wanted. One day, she grew frustrated with me and started signing everything she knew…milk, read, hungry, food, cracker, more, swing, shoes, on and on. I was devastated. Perhaps all our work, all those signs she "knew," really didn't have meaning yet, she was just an expert imitator. That same day, I read in a book that echolalia, or repeating back what you hear, is a very important step towards speech acquisition. We had gesture echolalia! This time, I saw my reading as a blessing—while we weren't as far as I thought, we were making progress.

Not long after I taught Sydney how to sign "more," I read about how to approach teaching sign as communication therapy. The author recommended absolutely *not* starting with the sign "more," because kids can get lazy and use it for everything. This was not the last time that our learning didn't quite keep up with our needs. I was upset to find out that we started out completely wrong. A few months after that, a private therapist I hired was upset because the sign we were using with Sydney for "bubble" looked too much like the sign for "ball" to her. I felt like we were taking two steps back for every one step forward. Thankfully, I soon came to realize that it was a trivial matter that we taught her "more" before specific nouns, and Sydney never needed to sign "ball." Sign language taught her the basic cause-and-effect nature of communication. As she progressed, she understood that words have meaning and that they can be used to communicate. With any therapy, it is easy to get caught up in the details. It feels good to be several years past her diagnosis and know that we are working on a big picture. We do the best we can and learn to be flexible about things. Therapy does not have to be perfect to be effective.

I suppose the best way to dig yourself out of a pile of dirt is to roll up your sleeves and get to it. I was intimidated about being the parent in charge of Sydney's therapy. I was in panic mode until the therapists from Easter Seals started coming into our home, showing me what to do. Just as soon as we started *doing* something, not only did I feel better about things, but Sydney responded, and we starting seeing amazing progress. It was as though the rain was letting up, clouds were parting and sunshine was breaking through the gray again.

Communication became my first priority for Sydney. I understood the need for speech therapy. After all, at the time of her diagnosis, Sydney had zero meaningful language or gestures, but what in the world was occupational therapy? I posed that question to my speech therapist and I can still hear her lovely Texas drawl: "I can't explain it to you, but my experience is that kids learn to speak faster if they are getting occupational therapy too." That was all I needed to hear.

Occupational therapy sounds, from its name, like something you need if you end up with a work-related injury. Occupational therapists help people learn or re-learn to do whatever it is that occupies the time of a person in that stage. For example, stroke victims are taught how to button clothes, tie shoes again, and take care of personal hygiene. Children are taught how to do the work of children—how to play. Occupational therapists also help a person live more independently and comfortably in his or her environment. I didn't understand it until we were doing it with our daughter.

I quickly become converted to the use of occupational therapy in addressing behavior issues with Sydney. Sydney was in an oral/motor play stage much longer than her neuro-typical peers. She put anything and everything in her mouth. In fact, the grosser the object, the more enticing it was to eat. One day, Sydney had a trail of white and red little round welts on her hand, traveling up her arm and around her mouth. Brian and I wondered what they could be, until the next day at the playground when I had to repeatedly pull her off of a fire ant mound—she was eating the ants. The week after Sydney's diagnosis, my mother-in-law flew out to stay with us. We got out of the car from picking her up at the airport and she held Sydney's hand as they walked into the house. A few feet from the front door, Sydney tore her hand away from my mother-in-law, bent over and picked up a bird dropping from off the sidewalk and popped it into her mouth. Welcome home, Grandma!

Perhaps it was the stress of a new baby in the house, or perhaps it was because I was behaving like a panicked mom, but something provoked more problem behavior in Sydney. She started eating her hair. In response to this, I trimmed her hair to just above her shoulders and cut some bangs to prevent her from getting the hair into her mouth. Now instead of just eating the hair around her face, she pulled out the hair from the top of her head and then ate it. I didn't so much mind her eating her hair, but I did mind that she was pulling out her already very thin hair. We tried unsuccessfully to stop it, but our efforts only increased my frustration.

I tried "extinction." Every time she started to pull out her hair, I pushed her little hand down and firmly said, "No." This always blew up into a power struggle. She screamed and pulled even more frantically at fistfuls of her hair, while I tried to muscle her hands away from her head. I spoke with one therapist about it, and she asked around at work and told me my only option was to cut off all of

Sydney's hair. I tried hard not to balk at her—WHATEVER! There was no way I was going to cut off the little bit of soft honey-brown hair my daughter worked two years growing! I was self-conscious already about her behavior; I was not going to make her *look* funny too.

One of the greatest problems for us at this stage was not knowing how long some of this strange behavior would last. We were projecting all her behavior problems 10 years down the road. Would Sydney have a bald head at age 15 from eating her hair?

I asked the occupational therapist for ideas. She had a different perspective. Sydney must really like either the sensation of pulling out her hair, or the sensation of having her hair in her mouth. If we gave her appropriate ways to have that sensation without actually pulling out her hair, maybe she would stop the behavior.

We decided to put her on a sensory diet that included a lot of oral motor play with string-like things. I bought beef jerky strips and cut them into thin threads. I gave her pieces of dental floss to put in her mouth. We went through a lot of licorice. The speech therapist gave us a vibrating teething toy. I gave her opportunities for string play during the day, and gave her a piece of beef jerky or dental floss anytime she started to pull out her hair. In several months, the behavior had become very infrequent, only surfacing when she was really tired. Eventually it turned into a ponytail twirling habit—and that was fine with me. That experience taught me a valuable lesson: experts are not right all the time. As Sydney's mommy, I can trust my feelings about her therapy. If I do not like what is going on, then there is probably a better way to accomplish something. That experience also endeared to me forever the profession of occupational therapy.

During this time, I was taking a parent-training course through the Texas "Any Baby Can" program. I met a wonderful woman whose daughter with autism was in her thirties. I told her about Sydney's hair pulling. Her reply really fascinated me. "Oh, my daughter did that too. She eventually stopped, Sydney will too, and then she will replace that behavior with something else that will drive you crazy."

I was relieved to hear someone offer reassurance that Sydney's behavior would not stagnate. Her statement was a mix of cynicism and honesty, hope and realism. As Sydney grew, she would progress, overcoming and meeting new challenges just as any person does. She might do it at a different pace than her peers, and her challenges might be of a different flavor, but she would grow and change just like her brothers or any other child. I was relieved to know that problems at two might not be problems at fifteen, but my friend's statement was also a reminder that there would probably always be something "different" about little Sydney.

My friend's words proved to be accurate. The hair eating was eventually replaced by hair twirling and hand biting. Then hand biting went away and her crying became more intense. And then her crying got better and she would "fake cry" saying, "Boo hoo! I am crying. Why are you sad?" Years later there was hand biting again— she had calluses on her fingers from her own teeth marks. There is and always will be a challenge to address! But with each new development, it became clear that Sydney's strength to control herself increases. She is not a victim, and we are not helpless.

Those first few steps we took in Texas were hard. With all the uncertainty, we were terribly vulnerable and we needed so much support. Fortunately, we had wonderful therapists who taught us basic principles and pointed us in the right direction. As we left

Texas, I felt uncertain about what we were to do next. Would the therapists in Ohio be as good as they were in Texas? After only a few months in Ohio, we felt confident that we knew what we needed to do. As her parents we could sense when a therapist was good or bad for her. Having taken the first few steps, we could advocate for our daughter.

Four months after Sydney's diagnosis, we left Texas for two weeks to visit family in Utah. At the time, I carried a counter around, keeping track of the number of words she said in a day. When we left Texas, with a lot of prompting, Sydney was using 10-20 words or signs a day. At the time we didn't care if they were meaningful or not. Upon our return two weeks later, she had increased to 70-100. After our move, by September of that year, just seven months after starting therapy, she had jumped to 400 signs or words in a day using 130 different words and 40 different signs.

One challenge in any personal experience account is trying to balance painting an accurate snapshot of reality with communicating a point. I want to share the hope that we have found, but I also realize that it can be very disheartening to read of someone's success with therapy when you yourself feel like you are beating your head against a brick wall. All throughout this account I focus on the positive things that happened with Sydney. I tell the happy stories, the success stories. Some things are easily resolved with the right intervention; other therapy goals have been pursued for years! There were just as many, if not more, not-so-successful attempts at therapy. No experience in my life has been as frustrating as trying to do therapy with Sydney and having it not work. Later, trying to do homework with Sydney was similarly difficult. Many days I got up to face the day determined to make a difference, and had Sydney totally ignore or resist my attempts. Equally frustrating were many therapy sessions that were thwarted or stopped completely by the needs of her brothers.

I wish I had a quarter for every time I had to sit back and take a deep breath, count to twenty, or say a prayer to keep from screaming or throwing something. I cannot count the number of times I ended up in tears, ready to quit entirely. I went through months at a time when I had to set a timer for 15 minutes to keep myself at a therapy task that long. This was so disheartening. I was ready to give up after two or three minutes. My goal for the day was to *just do it again*—I wasn't even expecting to see Sydney respond or react. I hung sticker charts on my front door with the therapy goals for each day of the week. One time I had a friend point to a goal and inquire, "So, Sydney gets a sticker when she will do this?" I said, "No, I get a sticker if I will attempt to get her to do it."

Many variables influence the effectiveness of therapeutic intervention. Some of the greatest challenges for us were knowing what to do, and then second-guessing ourselves constantly after we made a decision. That second-guessing can make it even more discouraging during times when progress is slow. We had periods when a two-minute therapy session was all we could handle in any one sitting.

The good news is that all those 2-minute sessions, all the 15-minute sessions added together made hours and hours of attention and interaction. The repetition, the routine, the predictability, the prayers, maybe even the weather patterns all eventually worked together, and Sydney made progress.

We have so many examples of breakthroughs with Sydney. When they happened, it was like a long night of darkness finally ending as morning started to crack through the slats of a shade. My journal is a stream of stories detailing disappointing periods when I thought a particular undesirable behavior would persist into adolescence, and then Sydney surprised us with a developmental leap.

One night while I was at a church function Brian was putting the kids to bed. On this particular night, he was at the end of his rope. He felt very guilty that Sydney ran in circles all evening and that he was cranky over the splashing and the buckets of water on the floor at bath time. He was upset about the general chaos and the total lack of control he felt. He put Sydney into bed, and out of habit said, "I love you Sydney." As he got up to leave she said back to him, "I love you too." He was so surprised. Neither of us had ever heard that before.

At one very dark point, we wondered if our Sydney would ever be capable of loving us. Many books paint such an ugly picture of autism—as though those individuals are incapable of loving other people. That just is not so. I believed the books for a long time, and it broke my heart. But then Sydney started improving, and it was easier to see how she showed us her love. She danced and sang and ran *toward* us, if not *to* us, when we picked her up from preschool. She calmed down if we (her parents) held her. She asked for us when we were gone. She sought us out when she wanted a book read or she wanted us to play with her. We know for certain that she does love us, and not just because she says it. With that said, because we are human beings, it is really nice to hear it—and that night, Brian did.

Sydney really struggled going to church in Texas; a room full of strangers, loud noises, big crowds, unfamiliar people looking at, speaking to, and touching her—it was total sensory overload. The move back to Ohio just made things worse. Week after week we wrestled with her as long as we could, and then removed her, screaming, from the meeting. One week I lost a button off the front of my dress because she was climbing up me, trying to get on top of my head. I took her outside, screaming and shaking. I wrapped her in her baby brother's blanket and tried swinging her in the parking lot. I finally strapped her into her car seat and stood next to the car until she fell asleep. Once she was asleep, a friend sat in the car with her while I led the music for the primary, which was my assignment at the time.

Trying to take Sydney to the church nursery was a total disaster. She bit her hands, screamed and cried buckets of tears. Brian and I prayed about what to do. As members of the Church of Jesus Christ of Latter-day Saints, going to church as a family is very important to us. I called the primary president, explained our problem, and then asked her if she would let Brian be a nursery worker. She consented (very enthusiastically) but even that didn't solve the problem. So, we wrote the "Church Book," a social story about what to expect at church. It was our first attempt at social stories—writing a story to help Sydney understand what to expect and how to behave. Sydney's episodic memory was not good. She did not necessarily remember the order things would happen; even if we did the same thing every week. We hoped the book would help her keep track of what to expect. To cater to Sydney's love for rhymes, we made it into a poem.

Church day, church day, yeah hurray!
Daddy will be home all day.
Here we go, 1, 2, 3...I'm as pretty as can be!
In the car, we drive, drive, drive. See the temple?
We've arrived!
In the chapel, we sit, sit, sit. Bread and water, just a sip!
Think of Jesus, sing a song, sit with Mommy, sure seems long!
Time for Nursery! Time to Play! Me and Daddy go our way.
Bye bye Mommy, Spencer too, you will come and see me soon!

Rebekah J. Shumway

In the room and close the door, see the table on the floor?
Time to color, cut and glue, here come kids to play with you!
Toy time! Toy time!
Open the door, kids spread toys across the floor.
Trucks and dolls and books and blocks,
Daddy says, "Keep on your socks!"
Smiley, smiley, laughy fun! Me and daddy run, run, run!
Clean Up! Clean Up! Clean Up fast! Bye bye toys, play time's past.
Time to close the great big door, spread the blanket on the floor.
Sit down, sit down, everyone! Look at pictures, fun, fun, fun!
Here comes song time! Sing, sing, sing! We can sing like anything!
Song time over, here we go! Make a line, go through the door.
Down the hallway, snack time now! Snack time, snack time, wow! Wow! Wow!
Hear the music, dance and move, let's blow bubbles!
Almost through.
Mommy! Mommy! Here she comes! Spencer, Isaac, nursery's done!
Bye bye nursery! Here we go! I love church days, let's go home.

We illustrated the book with photographs of people, activities and places at church. The week we took the pictures, Sydney was as distraught as ever. She was biting her hand and screaming in every picture in the book. I was worried that it might cue her to cry at church all the time, but it didn't. The book worked like a dream. The next week we read the book to her from the time she got up until we left for church, read it all the way to church, and then read it again in church. Although she still cried when it was time for nursery, she didn't scream inconsolably, and in a short period of time she calmed down and was fine for the rest of the class. She was two-and-a-half.

Once Sydney was four, she started to attend a different church class—the Sunbeams. We had to re-write the church book. The new Sunbeam church book did not have any photographs; Sydney's comprehension had improved to the point that we could use stickish cartoony pictures I drew with a marker. Previously, we had a terrible time getting Sydney to speak softly during sacrament meeting. She was happy at church now, but very loud. One verse said, "In the chapel, please sit still! Whisper, whisper while you're here." That next week, Sydney whispered for nearly half the meeting before her exuberance got the best of her. I couldn't believe it. We had told her hundreds of times to whisper, we signed "whisper," over and over, but once she saw the picture, and read it in her book, she finally understood it.

Using Social Stories for Sydney as a therapy strategy has been extremely effective. It continues to evolve over time. When she was in kindergarten, her teacher got extremely good at writing stories for her when issues arose. I knew what kind of day it had been by the social story in her backpack. Initially we used stories to help her anticipate something that would be hard; a change at school, going on a trip, having house guests, etc. Then the social stories became a behavior management tool, to address issues as they came up. I love social stories because they empower me. I feel like I am not helpless when Sydney is having a struggle with something. Most of the time the social stories have the format of:

1. Describing the problem
2. Illustrating that I understand how she is feeling.
3. Resolving the problem by showing Sydney how we would like her to behave.

One winter day, when Sydney was in the second grade, a blizzard had all the kids home from school. I don't know if it was the change in routine or the weather pattern itself, but Sydney was having a rough time. In addition to increased pacing and humming, she kept asking me over and over again if it was Valentine's Day. I became incredibly frustrated having to answer repeatedly. I knew she wanted me to tell her it was Valentine's Day—but we had just celebrated Valentine's Day. We had discussed in great detail when Valentine's Day is, that it had already passed, and that it would not happen again for a while. Finally, I grabbed a piece of paper and I wrote:

Once upon a time there was a sweet little girl named Sydney. She was fun, most of the time. But sometimes she would ask the same question over and over again. Then she was not so fun. She made everyone feel crazy.

"Is it Valentine's Day?" She asked.

"No." said her mother. "I know you like Valentine's Day. You had a fun party at school, didn't you?"

"Is it Valentine's Day?" She asked again.

"No. It is February 16th." replied her mother.

"It is Valentine's Day?" She asked again.

"Go to your room." said Mommy.

In her room, Sydney decided to stop asking about Valentine's Day. When she came downstairs she said,

"Let's paint a picture. Mom, I will help you wipe off the table."

"Thank you!" said Mom.

Everyone had fun painting. Sydney did not keep asking about Valentine's Day.

The End.

We read the story together a few times, and Sydney laughed about it. She quit asking about Valentine's Day. But when she finished wiping off the table to prepare to paint she said,

"Mommy, is it Groundhog Day?"

Sydney surprises us all the time with what she understands. She acts oblivious to her surroundings, and then she hops in and is right on cue. On my dad's birthday, I called him on the phone so we could wish him a happy birthday. I asked Isaac if he would sing Grandpa "Happy Birthday," and initially he refused. I found Sydney, humming and very absorbed in her dolls, and asked her if she could "say hello to Grandpa." She took the phone from me and sang "Happy Birthday to you, Happy Birthday dear Grandpa" perfectly, all the way through. I did not even realize that she heard me urging Isaac to sing. Her response made me wonder about how much of our conversations she understands, but we don't perceive it because she does not respond in the same way as her brothers.

All these experiences taught me that we could do a lot of things to help Sydney learn. We are not stuck, and things are not hopeless. In fact, we can have a lot of joy, and a lot of success. Autism does not have to stop her development; it just delays some of it. When Sydney was tiny, I enjoyed her slower growth. I enjoyed having a baby for a while longer. Babies are very hard to get, and they grow up too fast. Sydney's autism is a chance for me to enjoy her childhood just a little bit longer, and to thrill in the advancements of all my children a little more intentionally.

We moved from mourning our daughter's diagnosis to seeing rays of hope as we began therapy and saw her make small improvements. We felt empowered that we could do something for her. Her future was not as hopeless and dark as it originally seemed as we found things that could help our situation. The nighttime of our grieving passed, and the morning came. It was a new day for us—our life will never be the same, but overall, most of the change was improvement. We still had dark days with seemingly endless crying and cueing, and discouraging nights, but most of the time I wouldn't trade places with anyone in the world.

Rebekah J. Shumway

Gift 2: God's Tender Mercies

This book started out as an exercise for me in overcoming self-pity and depression. I was in an emotional rut, feeling very picked-on, and even a little resentful about Sydney's autism. One evening, I confronted my misery and determined to make some effort to overcome it. I decided to start a list of blessings that came out of our current life situation. I sat at my computer and said a prayer, "Help me see the good that has come from Sydney's autism." Then, I started making a list. The blessings came to mind slowly at first, and then I started warming up.

I reflected on the circumstances that surrounded some of the most difficult events in our lives, and tried to remember some of the good times. I started seeing flickers of light from the dark shadows of the painful memories. Soon, I was overwhelmed. I saw so clearly miracles that occurred in our behalf. Consequently, I started noticing the daily blessings that I had previously missed completely.

In all of the heartache and trial of our daughter's autism, it would be impossible to say that we have been abandoned or punished by God. In fact, the opposite is true. I have never seen evidence of His love for us or of His divine orchestration of our lives as I have with respect to our daughter's autism. We have been humbled and amazed on hundreds of occasions as we recognized the blessings that have been ours. I cannot begin to describe all the events of which I speak, but I must share some of the reasons why I know that God is mindful of us, that He loves our daughter, and that He is guiding our lives as we strive to help her grow.

Tender Mercy #1 — Our Community of Support

When Brian and I became engaged, he was right in the midst of interviews for dental school. When an invitation to interview in San Antonio came, I told him that if he went to dental school in Texas, I was going to graduate school in Utah and would marry him in 5 years when he was finished. I hate hot weather. I hate it so much that it makes me physically sick. Living anywhere in the South had as much appeal to me as moldy leftovers stuck in a gooey puddle at the back of the fridge. All I could think about when I considered Texas was the weather. Brian humored me and didn't interview in Texas at all; he passed it up and we ended up in Ohio. Four and a half years later, we were graduating from dental school and Brian was interviewing for residency programs. He had very strict criteria, and narrowed his search to just a handful of programs, one of which was in Texas. Upon his return from that interview, there was no other residency in the world for Brian. I have seldom seen my husband set his sights so certainly on anything. So, we moved to Texas in July. I was determined that I would endure one year, and it was going to be a tremendous showing of sacrifice and love on my part for my husband. I didn't realize at the time that it was a tremendous showing of God's love for us that He led us to Texas.

Among many changes, moving to Texas meant a new pediatrician, new ward, new friends and neighbors, and new work associates. All these changes were hard, but God carefully positioned our family to have the medical and social support we needed to get Sydney's diagnosis and get her started on a road to improvement. Looking back, many miracles facilitated her diagnosis. At the time, I couldn't see much blessing in all of it, but it became more apparent as

I learned of other families' struggles to get answers and help for a child with special needs.

We had not one, but two pediatricians who knew enough about developmental delays to see the red flags with our Sydney. At that time, many pediatricians do not recognize the signs, often delaying an appropriate diagnosis for years. For me, it was important that we lived in an area that had a center that did team evaluations. It was harder for me to argue with a diagnosis that was established by a panel of professionals. Additionally, it was a blessing that we got into the Village of Hope when we did. We were only in Texas a year, and their waiting list for an evaluation is often a year long.

The Village of Hope was my first exposure to professionals who work with children with special needs. Not everyone's first exposure is as good as mine was. I felt they carefully constructed an accurate perception of Sydney's abilities. I could not disregard their diagnosis with the argument that they didn't know our little girl. Had some of the circumstances surrounding her diagnosis been different, we may have delayed starting therapy, hoping for her to grow out of it on her own. God knows us individually. He knows that I am skeptical and doubting. He very carefully directed the events leading to Sydney's diagnosis to help me accept and act upon it.

The single most important factor that contributed to our successful beginning with Sydney was the help we received from therapists and staff at Easter Seals in San Antonio. After Sydney's diagnosis, we were referred to the State of Texas' Early Intervention program. Based on our zip code, we fell under the jurisdiction of Easter Seals. We loved the therapists from Easter Seals, and they changed our lives forever. God positioned us to meet the people we needed to meet to get the best help for Sydney. I have a favorite quote, "God does notice us, and he watches over us. But it is usually through another person that he meets our needs." (Spencer W. Kimball, *Ensign,* Dec 1974, page 2). Many people prepared us for the changes that we made to our lives to accommodate Sydney's autism. I mention a few to illustrate how God positioned us to have the support we needed.

When Sydney was first diagnosed with autism, one of the first people I thought to call was my speech therapist friend from Ohio. Interestingly, in addition to an aunt, I had three good friends who were speech therapists. I also had a friend who was an occupational therapist, and several others who were physical therapists. I made another phone call to a close friend whose brother has Asperger's Syndrome. They all were able to give me support, encouragement, some very important advice on navigating through the systems of special education, and some helpful lingo crash courses. I remember telling my sister some of the things they suggested, and she said, "Becky, I do not have *any* therapist friends." I was surprised. "Really? Seems like most of my friends are in special education somehow." As soon as I said it, I could see the miracle in it. God had, by no means, left us without help. He had been preparing me since high school to have friends who could help me with my new challenge.

God put us among a remarkable group of people in Texas who were instrumental in helping us adjust initially. Among our church friends in Texas, in our congregation of a few hundred was a family whose oldest boy had Asperger's Syndrome and youngest girl had spinal bifida. As I worked closely with their mother at church, I learned about coping with the stresses of having special needs kids. Watching them gave me a helpful glimpse of what could be in store for us. My friend helped replace some of my fears about the future with hope.

Rebekah J. Shumway

My first introduction to her children, ages 10, 8, and 6, was during a women's meeting at the church. I volunteered to work in the nursery, because I knew Sydney wouldn't let me leave her in the nursery with a stranger. When their mother brought them in, she asked me if I would let the boys run around the gym, because they were a little old for the nursery. Her daughter stayed and colored pictures with us. After her boys ran off to play, the mother said to me, "My oldest has autism, so sometimes it is a little hard to get his attention." I was curious. The boy seemed perfectly normal to me. When the meeting ended and refreshments were being served, the boys came to the nursery to get their sister. The oldest boy asked, "Can I take my sister and go eat a treat with our mom?" I told him he could, and his brother and sister laughed out loud. Then he did something I did not expect, he leaned over, picked her up and struggled to carry her back to their mom.

I was touched by their love and obvious enjoyment of each other. I thought, "Well, autism can't be all that bad!" Years passed before I came to appreciate fully this friend and the way she overcame struggles in her life. This woman continued to bless my life even after my association with her ended. She would probably be so surprised to know that she and her family had such an affect on me. While we lived in Texas, I did not consider her a close friend. We did not seem to have much in common. In fact, I even felt critical of her—she seemed overprotective and over-anxious to me. Only with the insight that comes with experience and time did I begin to reflect on our conversations and what I knew about her. I recognized the struggles she hid, masked in her optimism and cheery personality. I did not appreciate her friendship fully until we had moved from Texas and lost contact, but I continued to draw on memories of those conversations with her for years; they gave me great hope. We cannot predict who, in our circles of influence, will become our saving angels.

Over the years, there have been a lot of people I have admired, or at least I have admired a particular aspect of their lives. Most of the time, we don't get to know these people well enough to know their struggles—we only see their victories and are left with an incomplete and often idealistic impression. For example, in Texas I was introduced to a girl whose parenting skills really impressed me. She was one of the happiest moms I have ever met; she loved being a mom and loved being with her kids. She had three boys, ages 2, 4 and 6. She told me she didn't get out and socialize much because she didn't feel the need; she enjoyed the company of her kids. She played *with* her kids. She laughed out loud at the things they said, she talked to them like they were genuinely her friends. You could hear in the tone that she used that she really enjoyed them. Soft-spoken, intellectual, sincere and practical, she encouraged their curiosity and delighted with them in each little discovery.

One day, she called and asked if we would like to join them in planting a garden. I thought, "We are not going to be much help, but it sounds fun." It turned out, her goal was not really about getting help, the experience was all about being in the mud and letting the kids have a good time, and not about making sure we had straight rows or that the seeds were planted at the right depth.

The boys dug a big hole and filled it with water. Sydney sat right down in the middle of it, soaked to her chest in mud. The boys were so delighted. They kept yelling, "Look at the baby, look at the baby!" They treated Spencer and Sydney like their mother treated them, with love and attention and praise. We loved being with them, and I learned from her how to enjoy *more fully* the *process* of parenting.

Rebekah J. Shumway

As I got to know her better, I learned what you always learn about people you admire: things had not always been easy for her. She had struggled significantly at certain times. That just endeared her to me even more. I also learned that she got tired and sad and cranky too—just like the rest of us "regular" moms. We all have our dark days, weeks, months, or even years when we just can't seem to get things together. She offered valuable advice about what to do during those times, and encouragement to remember that those times are temporary.

Much later as we implemented therapy schedules, planned our playtime with objectives in mind, and tried to slow down and enjoy our relationships more, I was comforted as I thought of my friend. I was forced by our circumstances into doing what had appeared natural for her. Sydney needed mommy to play *with* her. Spencer, Sydney, and Isaac needed me to help them play together harmoniously. I had to slow down and enjoy the process in order to teach my kids the value of relationships, and to find joy and peace in my role as a mother. My life changed focus; it was not about a clean house, my hobbies, social groups, cooking meals, or physical fitness. My life was about enjoying my children for the fleeting, precious years they are young. My friend's depictions of that lifestyle made it seem doable and attractive. Initially I was overwhelmed with Sydney's therapy needs. With time, I was better at incorporating her therapy into everyday life. By engaging more actively with my children, I was not only helping them, but was increasing my own satisfaction and happiness. I was being transformed by Sydney's autism.

Once we moved back to Ohio, it became obvious that God had carefully positioned us once again. From her service coordinator to preschool teachers to the people supporting us at church, we felt we were blessed with people who were handpicked by God to be in our lives.

When she was nearly four, the time came to transition her with her nursery class into Primary and the Sunbeam Sunday school. Brian and I worried that she wouldn't handle it well, and we considered keeping her in the nursery longer, but decided to at least give Primary a try. We had support from so many people. The Primary president assigned a couple to her Sunbeam class, so one could teach while the other "helped" with sitting. Her teachers met with me and asked for ideas of things they could do to help her enjoy it more, and were very good sports about allowing Sydney to have a fidget toy, a snack, and a walk once in a while. The music director called and asked the same question. She used visual aids, signing, and incredible enthusiasm to make singing time wonderful for Sydney. The first weeks of primary, they sang songs she knew would be familiar to the new Sunbeams. Additionally, we wrote the "Sunbeam Book," and the combined efforts of everyone involved resulted in Sydney going to primary without incident, marching off with her older brother to Sunday school, no fussing at all. She quickly learned the songs and sang them around the house.

We have been touched by the love and acceptance people show Sydney. My first instinct was to hide her; to protect her from the mean world that would judge and scrutinize her. Our church family has taught us a very different viewpoint. After Sydney stopped yelling and screaming at church she flipped to the other extreme. She loved church. She wanted to sing and hum all through church. I was very conscious of her noise, and overly-sensitive about it. There is no cry room in an LDS church. I wanted her in the meeting with us—not roaming in the hallways for the rest of her life. I did not know if she would ever be quiet in church. One week she was particularly loud. She sang and sang while I tried desperately to keep her quiet. I was very frustrated and angry. Not angry that she was singing, but angry that my darling girl was so different—no other four-year old at church was singing during the sermons. When the intermediate hymn began, the woman in front of us turned around and said to me, "Please don't shush her. We love to hear her sing!" It was like heaven opened and God himself came down and held me. I started sobbing; the messy, noisy, heart-healing sort of crying.

We had a community of people who helped make church a happy, successful time for Sydney. I am so grateful for those people, for their love, dedication, kind words and patience.

God carefully positioned us to associate with people who could prepare us for what was coming with Sydney, and help us adapt our world for her. That became obvious in Texas, but our preparation for Sydney's diagnosis had started long before that.

Tender Mercy #2—Toys!

The Christmas after my mother died, when Sydney was nine months old, the family was gathered at home with my father. My brother Ben and his wife Sara gave my kids a six foot by four foot inflatable ball pit, complete with 100 plastic balls and ball-spitting inflatable fish. My first thought when we opened the gift was, "Oh, wow!" My second thought was, "What was Ben thinking?" And then, "Why didn't Sara stop him?" Brian and I laughed that Ben was out of touch with our lives. How were we going to get it home on the airplane? And then, where were we going to set it up in our 600 square foot apartment? Once home with the ball pit, it took Brian over an hour of huffing and puffing to set it up, and it took up all the space between our two sofas—you had to turn side-ways to walk from the front door to the kitchen. We could move the ball pit to the side, but even then it was a major piece of furniture. When company came over, we moved the ball pit upstairs, making the kid's room completely inaccessible. The ball pit, however, became our favorite toy. The kids loved it—both of them. Sydney was animated and interactive in the ball pit. She laughed at her brother and laughed at us. She shrieked with joy and babbled up a storm. We loved the ball pit because of the way it brought her out—and we did not even know about her autism yet.

The ball pit sustained some minor injuries in our move to Texas, and our enthusiastic love for it took its toll as well. Soon I was blowing up part of the ball pit every time the kids wanted to play in it, and it had a permanent place in our Texas apartment right in the front room.

A resident from Brian's work, whose family was in construction, suggested putting foam pipe insulators in the sides that had leaks. This worked really well until most of the ball pit was foam insulator stuffed, and then it did not have the structural integrity to remain upright. But Sydney and Spencer still loved it. They played in it alone and together, they climbed in it for comfort and for fun. At one point, I had something stinking in my front room and I finally decided it must be the ball pit. Sure enough, after some digging I discovered a rotting bottle of milk that started to blow from the pressure. The balls got a swim in some dishwasher detergent in the bathtub, but the ball pit took a short trip to the dumpster. I couldn't bear the thought of being without a ball pit, so the balls were put in an inflatable swimming pool in the front room. Eventually that too was destroyed, and the balls ended up in a six by six foot inflatable bouncer that ate up a large part of the master bedroom.

Rebekah J. Shumway

One day, at the start of a speech therapy session, Sydney's speech therapist said, "I read some research that says kids with autism respond very favorably to speech therapy done in a ball pit." I laughed. I could have told her that! "Wait till you see what I have in the bedroom," I said. We rolled the inflatable bouncer to the front room and re-loaded it with the plastic balls for speech therapy that day.

Looking back, we had hundreds of hours of therapy with Sydney in that ball pit. We did not know it was therapy, to us it was just play. To her, however, it was a bridge to our world, where she could comfortably cross and be with us for a moment before returning to the confinement of her solitary play. Ben may have been out of touch with our lives, but he wasn't out of touch with God, and God knew we needed a ball pit.

Therapy requires a lot of toys. Children learn through play, and those with autism are no exception. However, these children are not always inclined to play; often you first must structure their play so it is desirable, and then show them what to do. Designing playtime using games, toys, and strategies that teach a certain concept or provide a specific type of movement opportunity is a constant challenge in creativity. We have been humbled repeatedly as we see the ways the Lord provides precisely what we need, even in the smallest details.

During one of our first sessions with our occupational therapist, she pointed out that Sydney did a lot of running back and forth, up and down the hallway, and that she did a lot of pacing in small circles. She hypothesized that Sydney was doing this because it was giving her sensory feedback of some kind that she liked or needed. She suggested that as part of Sydney's sensory diet, we try swinging her in a blanket to give her more vestibular input. She brought a blanket that she laid on the floor, and then we put Sydney inside and we both picked up an end and started swinging her. Sydney loved it! She squealed and immediately relaxed. When we tried to stop, she wouldn't get off the blanket, she wanted more. The therapist showed me how to use the swing to help Sydney focus on a task, calm down, elicit communication, or heighten her awareness.

Soon afterwards, Sydney awakened in the middle of the night in a screaming fit. Brian and I went into her room, put her into a blanket and started slowly rocking it back and forth. She immediately calmed down. In a few minutes, she was ready to go back to bed. We were amazed. The only trick came when Brian was at work and I had to swing her in a blanket myself. For the reader who is trying to imagine this, it is as tricky as it sounds. I spread the blanket on the rug, had the child lie on the blanket, and then collected up the corners of the blanket in my hands and swung it back and forth in front of me or between my legs. Swinging Sydney was not terrible work, but her three-year-old, 40 pound older brother wanted in on the fun, and I didn't think there was any way I could explain to him that I would swing his sister and not him! I attempted to rig up some less strenuous ways of swinging them that would not be as hard on my back and arms. I tried tying an end of the blanket to the leg of the futon, but the stationary end made it more of a shaker than a swing.

Just a few days later, we were playing at the park and I was visiting with a friend who was looking at an Ikea catalog. I had never heard of Ikea, so she insisted I peruse it for a minute. I started thumbing through the catalog, looking at furniture and commenting on it for politeness' sake. Then I saw it—an Ikea swing. The swing was designed for indoor use, and it looked like a laundry bag suspended by a ceiling bolt. I was ecstatic. I went home that night and started making our swing. I didn't know how the property manager would feel about us installing a bolt into the ceiling of our apartment that could hold up to 200 pounds, so instead we purchased a chin-up bar at a sporting-goods store. Soon, we had a swing that hung in the kid's bedroom doorframe. Sydney loved it. The motion made a huge difference in her demeanor, often immediately. Many nights I sat on the floor in the dark and pushed her in the swing until she fell asleep. Spencer loved it too! We learned the "bad parent" way to be careful the kids didn't end up slamming into the doorframe. In addition to the back and forth movement, we could change the direction of the swing and even twist it up to spin it for them. Sydney and Spencer fought over who got to be first and then cried when they had to come out. The swing was a miracle.

Sydney's sensory needs changed as she grew. Eventually, swinging was just for fun, just like other kids. One occupational therapist explained to me that as their central nervous systems mature, they crave and dislike new things. Life is a continual adventure trying to identify and respond to Sydney's sensory needs.

The swing and the ball pit are just two examples of therapy toys that made a difference in Sydney's development. Toys for therapy can be expensive, especially when therapy requires such a variety, but we continue to be blessed by garage sale and thrift store finds, inspired hand-me-downs and thoughtful presents from family members and friends. God continues to provide tools of the trade to help our daughter, and frequently He provides them before we even realize we are in need! God didn't stop at just the equipment; He also prepared us for Sydney's autism through my education.

TENDER MERCY #3 — STATISTICS 100

So, what does chemical engineering have to do with behavioral science and special education? Aside from the fact that engineers have their own brand of social peculiarities, it wouldn't seem as though there is much in common. Once, in the midst of grappling with all the information we received about autism, I thought, "In 220 college credits, surely I could have thought to take some sort of child development or human development class!" Nope. Up until then, most of my child development had been learned at the playground or talking on the phone with my accountant sister. I did not foresee how useful my engineering degree and my background would be.

Starting in high school, every job I ever had could fit into two categories: janitorial or research, but mostly research. Research jobs were interesting, had flexible hours, and paid better than other college jobs. I did marketing research in high school, and then I did carpet testing research, insect cell culture research, combustion research, and thermodynamic property research. Because of my experiences, I took a statistics class in college on research design. Once I graduated, I took a job doing business risk management, using more of my statistics than chemistry background. I would have never believed that those jobs and that class would be important once I was a full-time homemaker, but they have proven to be extremely valuable.

How do parents decide what kind of therapy to do with their child? It is overwhelming to see the scope of choices available and terrifying to read all the books claiming that their way is the most effective, and that if you don't do it their way, you are shortchanging your child's future. Having the ability to understand the statistics of research proved to be essential. In the beginning, I knew next to nothing about behavioral science, but I could pick up a study and make basic conclusions about the strength of the results based on sample size, possible confounding variables and whether or not the results had been replicated. I discovered that behavioral science research is very hard to do well. It is impossible to get the accuracy and the dependability that you get out of other kinds of research. For instance, how do you isolate variables in an autism study? Parents who allow their children to be in an autism study are normally very involved in autism intervention, and they are rarely implementing exclusively the therapy in question. Not many parents are going to stop all other kinds of therapy to focus on just one. The children with autism I have known receive numerous therapies, and are simultaneously on health supplements of some kind along with restrictive diets. Additionally, regardless of therapy, children with autism gain some skills as they mature just like their non-autistic peers. How does one know that improvement in a child is from a therapy in question, and not due to another factor?

It is a very difficult thing to evaluate therapy and to know what is effective. Early on in Texas, I implemented a strict diet with Sydney. I tried it for two weeks and abandoned it because the soymilk I put her on gave her diarrhea. (Or maybe it wasn't the soymilk—maybe she would have had diarrhea even without the soymilk. We will never know.) In that next month, we saw dramatic improvement. I observed out loud to my husband that if we had stuck to that diet, I would have thought the diet contributed to Sydney's success during that time. When in fact, she made those improvements without the diet.

Sometimes you find exactly the right therapy, diet, or whatever for a child that will help them immensely; sometimes kids make improvements just because they are getting older. It is very hard to isolate the variables and nail down exactly why one child improves, while another one doesn't.

I heard a hundred times during my coursework in engineering that we were learning how to problem-solve. My husband pointed out that I approached Sydney's autism like an engineer. I wanted to know what all the variables were, what their values were supposed to be, and what needed to be done to fix them. After the initial shock wore off, I worried less about the fact that she had autism, and more about the individual components of her autism. For instance, through focusing on her sensory integration disorder (e.g. her craving of vestibular input), we could identify specific strategies to address her weaknesses (e.g. swinging her several times a day), and consequently we saw remarkable improvement (e.g. she didn't run in circles as much and was easier to calm). A large problem resolves more quickly when it can be divided into smaller problems that can be addressed one at a time.

Additionally, this approach has been helpful to me emotionally, because it forces me to focus on things that improve more quickly than the overall picture. Hanging a swing in the doorway didn't cure her autism, but we did have a very powerful tool for calming her and helping her focus.

I didn't study engineering or learn the statistics of research thinking that they would be valuable skills to have as a mother. When I was making those decisions, I was not married and did not have special education on my radar at all. It has been fascinating and humbling to realize that God prepared me for Sydney's autism long before I knew anything about it. He really does orchestrate our lives—preparing us during Act I for what is going to happen in Acts II and III. Some of putting our trust in the Lord is simply acknowledging the goodness He has already shown us, and recognizing the miracles that happen every day.

Rebekah J. Shumway

Tender Mercy #4 — A Tight Budget

Sydney's autism diagnosis and the first three-and-a-half years of her early and intensive intervention came during my husband's post-graduate residencies. When Sydney was diagnosed with autism, we had Isaac sleeping in the walk-in closet of our bedroom and we were drinking powdered milk to make our grocery budget stretch. We had a huge student loan balance, and we owed my father money for help he gave us to buy a car that would fit three car seats in the back. After I started reading about what was recommended for children like her I panicked: one-on-one therapy for six to eight hours a day, five days a week, hiring therapists to come into your home, speech therapy, occupational therapy, music therapy, therapeutic listening therapy, equestrian therapy, animal therapy — the list seemed endless. There was no way we were going to be able to pay for that! We were going to have to do it differently.

I am so grateful now for our poverty then. It forced me to thoroughly research our therapy options. I wanted to be certain we were doing the best thing for Sydney before we invested our limited funds. I read books about therapy; I read the original research about specific therapies. I read the critiques and the rebuttals. I attended conferences. As a result of my research, I am not as easily swayed by grand claims and the emotional case studies. We make decisions based on my research, and then we "tweak" the therapy to fit our budget and our lifestyle.

We had weekly sessions for Sydney with both an occupational and a speech therapist. During those sessions I took notes and asked questions and then I tried to repeat those sessions every day for the next week. The therapists provided wonderful expertise and goal setting that I could not do myself. They were encouraging and optimistic as they taught me how to work with my daughter. However, even with those components we worried, "Are we doing enough?" We looked around into additional kinds of therapy.

We implemented a play and ABA (Applied Behavioral Analysis) based therapy routine for the first nine months after Sydney's diagnosis. However, we didn't hire a consultant at $150/hour and then train our own therapists at $10-$15 hour. I met three times with a consultant, purchased a manual, evaluation packets and score sheets, evaluated her myself, goal-set myself, and then implemented therapy each day myself. I was uncomfortable with the rigidity of the therapy: I made a lot of changes to make it more enjoyable for me and for her. We didn't do it exclusively: we also incorporated sensory integration therapy, traditional speech therapy and our own brand of relationship therapy. It was exhausting and all consuming, and it probably didn't happen as consistently as it would have had we hired people to do it for us, but it was successful. Sydney made significant progress, but she wasn't the only one progressing. I progressed. Spencer progressed.

One of the most powerful tools we discovered for Sydney was a picture schedule. I laminated a poster board and then stuck a Velcro strip on it. Then I took pictures of all the different types of activities we did during the day: getting dressed, eating, riding bikes, going to the park, table time (with flashcards and such) etc. We found a way to represent with a picture everything we might choose to do, and the places we would normally go. Each night I would prepare the picture schedule for the next day. What would we do? It was all spelled out from eating breakfast to going to bed at night. It drastically reduced the anxiety and the tantrumming Sydney struggled with. To our surprise, our boys needed it too. Everyone was so much happier and cooperative with the picture schedule.

When Spencer was about three months old, Brian's grandmother asked me if I had the baby on a schedule yet. I replied sarcastically, "Yes, when he is tired, he sleeps, when he is hungry, I feed him." I hated the idea of a schedule. I was never good about schedules. Three years later, I had to live by an activity schedule that spelled out exactly what we did all day long. It was an intense exercise in acquiring skills in discipline, organization and planning that I had never anticipated. Had I been able to hire someone to do it for me, I would have missed out on substantial personal growth.

Eventually the ABA based therapy was not the best thing for Sydney, and we switched to Dr. Stanley Greenspan's Floortime® program and Dr. Steven Gutstien's Relationship Development Intervention®. We approached these programs the same way we approached the ABA therapy; I read the books, attended conferences and lectures, perused the websites and then did my best to implement the methods myself around our entire family's needs, making constant adjustments.

Another blessing that has come from our extensive involvement has been the ability to evaluate the effectiveness of the programs we try. My personal experience has been that if the parent is not the one doing a considerable amount of the therapy, it is hard to know how effective the therapy is. It is also hard to know why it is or isn't working. This is true even when the parents are involved all the time—but it is compounded when they are not around to see the actual interactions.

Doing Sydney's therapy with her helps me grow. I learn more about her, I learn more about me, I learn more about Spencer and Isaac. It also bonds her to me. For children who have a hard time forming relationships, I believe that having a parent constantly involved in therapy provides a sense of security and a model for future relationships. In the beginning, I felt I was the last person on earth qualified to help her; but I was the only full-time therapist we could afford! Later I learned that just the opposite was true—I was the person *best* qualified in the world to help her.

Not everyone will find success in the model of what we did. There is no way to give a child with autism what they need without help from trained professionals. They are an invaluable resource! Many things can contribute to how much help a family will need in implementing a therapy program for a special needs child. Large families, health concerns (emotional and physical) of parents, and families with multiple children with special needs are going to need outside help for larger pieces of the therapy load. Each family needs to carefully consider what they need and how they will go about getting those needs filled.

In every situation, parents need to try to understand the theory behind whatever therapy they are doing. It matters less *what* they decide to do than it matters that they understand *why* they are doing it. A parent must understand the theory so changes can be made to a program to fit the individual needs of a child. Parents need to be the driving force, the decision makers, the advocates, and the experts on their child and their needs. I do not think it is effective to acquiesce those jobs to others—the price is too high, and I don't mean economically.

In spite of our inability to hire help, we did not have to go about things alone. Between three of my sisters and my mother-in-law, I had live-in help on and off for 7 of the first 18 months following Sydney's diagnosis. Shortly after we started Sydney's therapy, my college-age sister, Emily, came to live with us for the summer. She came to help with our upcoming move, the new baby, and Sydney's therapy. Her presence was crucial during a very crazy period. She gave me the time I needed to do some intense studying and goal setting. It was a wonderful experience to have substantial time with my sisters and my mother-in-law. It deepened my love and appreciation for them, and increased my children's bond with them. It helped me feel less alone.

Having my life fill up with therapy helped me redefine my priorities as a stay-at-home mom. After Emily returned to college, I was overwhelmed. Once when I was talking to my dad on the phone, he offered to hire a housekeeper for me. What a great idea! It does not matter who scrubs your toilets or folds your laundry. But it does make a difference who is teaching your child how to trust, love, and enjoy communication.

Our approach was to use professional therapists for weekly or monthly sessions with Sydney and to act as ongoing consultants. I agonized over putting Sydney in preschool. By that time, we had a very structured, goal-oriented play environment at home. I even had the audacity to ask a representative from the county's MRDD (Mental Retardation and Developmental Disabilities) agency what they could give Sydney at school that I couldn't give her at home. He very graciously told me, "Not much. You already run a preschool here." My husband and I decided that we wouldn't do preschool, we would hire private speech and occupational therapists on a weekly basis and I would continue working with her at home. After fighting almost a year with our insurance, we were denied coverage for occupational therapy and given enough coverage for less than two months of speech therapy services in a year.

At the time, Brian was moonlighting one Saturday morning a month at a local dental clinic. He and I decided that he would start working every Saturday to come up with the $800-$1,000 a month we would need to cover both the speech and occupational therapy. Just a few days after we made that decision, Brian lost his job. For the first time in my life, I was very angry with God.

We decided to look into the preschool option because it was a way to have access to the speech and occupational therapy expertise. The local school district had a program we could access for free. The cost was right, but I was very skeptical. From what I had read, I was certain I would hate it. But, we were desperate, so I made an appointment for us to observe in the classroom that had an opening for Sydney.

Brian and I were both completely changed. We were so impressed. We fell in love with the classroom, the six other children, and the teacher's aide and speech therapist that were there that day. They were warm and gentle, happy and enthusiastic. They laughed with the kids and with each other. It was a lovely experience. I went into the room, certain I would find major faults that would make it unacceptable for my baby girl, but that just didn't happen. As we were leaving, the coordinator from the county turned to me and said, "I would trust any of my children to the women in this classroom." I believed her.

At subsequent meetings, and then after Sydney started attending, I was even more convinced that Sydney was in the right place. I stood in the hallway outside the classroom and spied on her through the windows. Even in the very difficult beginnings, the teachers were gentle, kind, and paid the individual attention she needed. They were thrilled with her accomplishments, like she was theirs. They loved her, and we loved them. I couldn't believe our good luck.

For a year I had structured the therapy I did for Sydney around what I watched her private therapists do once a week. I simply copied and then elaborated on the games and skills they focused on during their sessions. I wanted private speech therapy in addition to preschool—mostly for my benefit. Because my insurance would not cover it, I went to the graduate student Speech-Language-Hearing Clinic at Ohio State University. Because they were students in training, I could get an hour of speech therapy for a fraction of the cost.

This was a great investment. The students were eager and fresh, and full of great ideas. Many of them were willing to prepare handouts for me that I could take notes on during their sessions. I didn't worry about quality—their work was closely supervised and scrutinized. The supervisors were wonderful to work with. Sydney went through close to a dozen different therapists. Initially I was concerned, because I wondered if the frequent therapist changes would thwart therapy. But that is not what we experienced. We were sad each time a therapist had to move on, but each subsequent one had a new perspective and new ideas. We loved the student clinic.

At the time Brian lost his job, it looked like God turned his back on us. We had prayed about our decision to not put Sydney in preschool. We went to the temple and we fasted about it. We made a decision that felt right, and then the financial floor fell out of our plans. I was so angry! As usual, God reciprocated with love and blessings. If we could have afforded private therapy we would not have placed Sydney in preschool or used the student clinic; but preschool was exactly what she needed, and the clinic turned out to be a gold mine of ideas for me. God led us where we needed to be in spite of ourselves through the blessing of our poverty.

Sydney's preschool experience was wonderful for our family. For two-and-a-half hours a day she was in an engaging, attentive, and developmentally appropriate learning environment that I didn't have to orchestrate. Those precious hours were spent running errands, spending time with my boys, napping, and recharging—without any guilt!

We found the therapists employed by the school district and at Ohio State to be valuable resources. Her progress would certainly have been slower without them. However, as helpful as they were, the bulk of what was done for Sydney was done at home. I think the burden of helping a child overcome the barriers of special needs lies primarily with the parents.

I have had only a few negative experiences with professionally trained therapists, but those few sessions were very frustrating for Sydney and the therapist, as well as for me. One in particular convinced me that I am often better off doing it myself. The therapist was set on her lesson plan and determined to get through it with Sydney, and she had a totally inappropriate tone with her. She was very easily frustrated by Sydney's lack of response, and grew agitated and sharp.

Many families hire students and train them as therapists to try to reign in the costs. Therapists are hard to train. It takes a lot of time and effort, and even then you are not guaranteed that they are going to do things the way you'd like them to. Housekeepers are normally easier to train and less expensive. Now, when I am feeling overwhelmed, I think, "Well, hire a housekeeper!" it helps me keep perspective on what is important. Anything that a housekeeper can do is not the most important thing on earth. So, dishes pile up in my sink, laundry sits for days, unfolded on the couch, and mold grows in my toilets; but my babies and I play.

It is hard as a mom to take a day off, but that is how I survived all the demands of what went on every day. Every month or so, I checked out a good book from the library, and for two days I sat on the couch and read, let the kids run wild, forgot about doing therapy, and just put out the big fires. At the end of those couple of days, it took a few more days to dig out of the laundry, dish, and toy situation, but I was ready to tackle life again.

Personal growth and more accurate evaluations are not the only reasons I am glad we were forced into being Sydney's main therapists. Another important reason is that I am able to include Spencer and Isaac in Sydney's therapy. Paid therapists may not include siblings since time spent with your other children is time they are not spending with your special needs child. From the beginning, I felt it was healthy for Sydney to have to take turns and learn to interact with her brothers. It is also totally impractical to do hours and hours of one-on-one therapy with a child when there are other children. Sometimes, we see progress made just in allowing normal family interactions to occur.

In our home, therapy time is not just about Sydney. Sometimes Spencer and Isaac participate as therapists, asking questions and giving directions. Sometimes they participate as patients—anxious to answer the silly questions or play the new games. I have so many precious memories of Spencer, Isaac and Sydney working with me on some aspect of Sydney's therapy. The boys have been wonderful comrades in arms. I would have missed out on substantial relationship development opportunity and very sweet memories if we could have afforded the therapists I felt I needed early on.

TENDER MERCY #5—HURRAY FOR SIBLINGS!

The Gift of Autism

One of the most obvious blessings we have had from the very first day we held Sydney was her brother, Spencer. Spencer had a keen ability to connect with Sydney. I think some of it came from participating in hours of therapy with her, coaxing, begging, and tricking her into talking. Some of it came from hearing us talk and pray about it. But some of it was hardwired in him even before we knew anything was wrong.

I would not be surprised if when life is over we discover that they were good friends before they came to earth, and he was sent along ahead of her to be her guardian angel. Spencer adored Sydney and included her in whatever he was doing from the time he was 17 months old. For several years, Spencer was the only person who could make her laugh. They were special friends from the moment he first kissed her in the hospital nursery. It's a long told lament that kids don't come with instruction books, but God sent Sydney to us with her own private therapist. Spencer has a special sister, and he has always seemed to know it.

When Spencer was four, he and I worked with Sydney for a long time to try to get her to match objects to pictures during our table therapy time. She was terrible about doing it consistently, even though I thought she was perfectly capable of it. After months of this, one day she did the first set of cards perfectly, unprompted, on the first try. Spencer was so excited, he said, "This is going much better today than it did yesterday, isn't it Mommy?" Spencer's help was not just confined to formal therapy time.

Siblings are a natural source of harassment, and that can be strong incentive for communication. One night at dinner, Spencer accidentally picked up Sydney's bread and started eating it. We had guests for dinner, and the kids were eating at a small table. Sydney got up from her chair and came to the adult table and said, "Bread,

bread, please, please." I looked and saw that Spencer had her bread so I asked him to give her the other piece on his plate. She heard me talking to him about his bread so she turned to him and said, "Share, share, please." We had not previously ever heard Sydney use the word "please" combined with a request on her own.

Spencer didn't have to be coerced into including his sister. Once, when I was leaving to run errands I explained to Spencer that Daddy was upstairs working, and that he could watch his video while I was gone. I picked up Sydney and Spencer said, "Why does Sydney have to go?" I said, "So Daddy doesn't have to keep her out of trouble while I am gone." He said, "I promise I will watch her very careful. I promise Mommy. If she does anything bad, I will go get Daddy." So, I left her for Spencer to tend. I think it is not uncommon for the siblings of special needs kids to get an extra helping of that responsibility trait.

We have video footage of Spencer and Sydney decorating a cake. Sydney wouldn't stop wiping the frosting off the cake with both hands and eating it. Eventually, my sister had to take Sydney into the kitchen to clean her up, and Spencer was left at the table with the cake and a spatula. He carefully fixed the places she messed up and said to the camera, "Anytime Sydney messes anything up; I just try to fix it, if I can. If I can't, I just get Mommy or Daddy to fix it." Spencer was four, and he was already consciously fixing her messes.

Watching home videos, we can relive precious moments when Sydney is normal, when she is laughing at Spencer or enjoying something with him. It was as though Spencer was trained in Heaven how to be her therapist. It took conferences, dozens of books, professional therapists, and practice for Brian and I to learn how to reach her, but Spencer knew how to from the beginning.

THE GIFT OF AUTISM

Sydney's luck with siblings did not stop with her older brother. Twenty-three months after Sydney was born, Isaac entered our home. Isaac was such a treat for us. Initially, Sydney ignored her new brother. More than once I caught her standing on his back after I put him on the floor, acting like he wasn't underneath her feet. Once we were trying to teach Sydney our family names, we were all surprised when "Isaac baby" was the first name she mastered. She could identify our pictures on a flash card, but Isaac's name was the first she ever used to refer to someone.

We anticipated that Isaac would eventually pass up his sister developmentally, we did not expect that to happen at three months old—but it did. We have been so amazed by Isaac. Isaac is special; but we are also hyper-aware of what a miracle it is to see a human grow. He is a blessing to his sister for hundreds of reasons, and one of those is his teasing that has forced Sydney into communicating her frustration.

Sydney and Isaac had a love/hate relationship. They wanted to be involved with each other, but they were in each other's space all day long. This relationship enabled emotional growth and expression of feelings that would have been hard to duplicate without Isaac.

I have been surprised at Sydney's ability to imitate a behavior months after she's seen it. Right after we moved back to Ohio, I went through a time of thin patience with Spencer. He was very demanding, and had a skill for getting into trouble without actually doing anything technically wrong. I was short-tempered with him, and frequently when I was, we played a game. I said very calmly, "Spencer, do you know how it makes me feel when you (insert newest creative infraction?)" He'd laugh and say, "No." and then I would say, "It makes me feel like roaring like a lion!" I would then let loose on a terrible roar. It got Spencer's attention and made the ensuing why-is-that-a-bad-idea talk more effective, and it helped me blow off some steam without hurting feelings or bodies.

Several months later, my sister was with Sydney in the kitchen and Isaac was trying to climb up onto Sydney's stool. Sydney started with the normal panicked, "Isaac, Isaac, Isaac!" and then she turned and held her hands to her face and she roared like a lion. Isaac laughed at her. I couldn't believe it, but I saw it a few days later. Isaac was trying to close the closet where Spencer and Sydney were playing. Sydney said, "Isaac, Isaac, Isaac…ROOAAR!" I was thrilled. She remembered from *months* ago how I roared at Spencer, but more importantly and amazingly, she understood *how I was feeling* when I roared, and she knew that she was feeling the same way about Isaac.

Isaac has also been a wonderful playmate—when he was two years old and Sydney was four, he and Sydney were equal developmentally in many ways. Games that grew tiresome to Spencer after twenty or so repetitions were still entertaining to Isaac, so Sydney continued to have a comrade. We also observed Isaac copying Sydney and vice-versa. Sometimes the distinction between who is the older sibling blurs among the two of them. Whenever I had the two of them in my double stroller, it was not uncommon for people to inquire about my twins.

Even at barely two-years-old, Isaac helped me with Sydney, whether it was really helpful or not. For instance, after speech therapy I had to pay for the session and get verbal instructions from the speech therapist for the coming week. While I was paying, the kids sat in chairs in the waiting room to keep them from running wild everywhere. Sydney went through a phase of thinking it was very funny to run away from me. She'd get up and run away, and then little Isaac would run after her and drag her back to the waiting room. It looked a little funny, toddler Isaac a good three inches shorter than

Sydney, his pudgy arms wrapped around her chest, pulling her back into the room while he said, "Come back, Sydney. Come back, Sydney."

Finding balance between giving a special needs child the therapy they need, and still having a normal family life with time left for the needs of other children is really hard. Children are perceptive and they are experts at sensing changes to the dynamics of a family, and this creates some interesting challenges. Early on, Spencer caught on very fast to the program that "if-Sydney-signs-for-it-then-she-gets-it." Several times I caught him with Sydney cornered, signing like crazy and saying, "Sydney, do you want a cookie?"

We went through times when Spencer and Isaac acted up over the attention that Sydney needed. As a precocious 5-year-old, Spencer grew frustrated with the same games repeated hundreds of times, and Isaac's two-year-old eagerness was often destructive. Extremely helpful and very enthusiastic, they were both also my main hindrance to therapy time with Sydney on more than one occasion. With that considered, it was healthy to stop once in a while and throw therapy out the window while we focused on what the boys wanted to do. I found that if my attitude and my balance were right, then we had fewer problems with the boys feeling frustrated. Still, therapy that was hard to do with Isaac participating was done during his naptime. This also helped establish a routine for the older kids. For Spencer, the best way for me to avoid frustrating him was to include him in what we were doing. It worked best if I explained very clearly what we were going to play and why, and then explained his role.

For a while, I had trouble about half of the time with Spencer acting up during Sydney's therapy time. Frequently, I got very agitated with him. Once, when he was expressing frustration over playing a game a certain way that I had devised to accomplish a therapy objective, I sent him to his room and told him that he would lose his friends if he continued to be a bad sport. Spencer immediately started crying and he asked if his friends would die if he were a bad sport. I felt so badly, and upon reflecting on the circumstances, realized that it would have been fine to tweak things in a way that would have made the game more interesting for Spencer while maintaining the objectives for Sydney. Sometimes Sydney is not the only one who is too rigid in routines.

This lesson took some time to learn. In the beginning, when things were so scary and new and Isaac was tiny and sleeping a lot, I was not as good about pulling Spencer in and including him. The more time I spent with Sydney, the more Spencer worked at vying for my attention, good or bad. Finally, I realized I was missing a valuable asset in Spencer, and I was pushing him away from me. I decided it was better for things to slow down and include Spencer, than for things to be more efficient while Spencer felt badly for being scolded or excluded. I learned that when Spencer was clamoring for attention or hindering therapy attempts, I tried to think, "Pull him close, don't push him away." I stopped and listened to what he wanted to say, I let him run it his way once, I took the time to explain what we were trying to do, and I tried to physically and emotionally pull him in. When he was getting the positive attention he needed, I did not have to give as much negative attention.

Kids can act up anytime there are major family changes; Sydney's autism and Isaac's birth occurring together turned life upside down for Spencer. He decided that he wanted to be like Isaac and Sydney. He wanted to do all the naughty things that Sydney did (like jump on the couch and put his hands in his water glass at dinner), and he wanted us to warm up his milk before he would drink it (to be like Isaac). I had that "being a baby isn't all it is cracked up to be" talk with him. Finally, I realized the real issue was the special attention his siblings got. I decided that if warming his milk helped him to feel loved, then that was a small price to pay.

During that period, I started doing pre-school time with Spencer to try to balance all the attention Sydney was getting. I bought a preschool workbook, and let Sydney color at the table while I worked with Spencer. I tried not to worry when she didn't color. Often she just played with the crayons or sat in her seat humming or singing to herself. I reminded myself that this was Spencer's time, and as long as she was safe and happy, it was okay. Spencer loved it, and it helped him to feel that he had his special time too.

Giving one-on-one time to Spencer and Isaac proved to be very important. Preschool for Sydney was a blessing, not just because she got help from occupational, physical and speech therapists, along with her special education teachers, but also because it gave me a few hours in the afternoon to give special attention to Isaac and Spencer. It paid significant dividends for me to set aside time to play with my boys. My mother used to say that relationships with kids are like bank accounts, you have to deposit more in the account than you withdraw.

Letting Spencer help with everyday chores was a wonderful way to pull him close. It allowed him to feel like he was getting special attention, and it got some housework done! Often, it worked to engage Sydney too. Helping gave both a sense of belonging and of teamwork, and it taught responsibility.

It also made just switching the laundry a 15 minutes affair. Learning to slow down and let my life with my kids take a little longer has been a valuable lesson. After all, it is not about how fast we get the laundry done, it is about the experiences we share.

When I can, I make therapy as innocuous as possible—hiding it in games and pretend play. For instance, flash cards are a great way to practice a skill early on, but both Spencer and Sydney grow tired of flash card time. One day I spread 10-15 flash cards out on the floor face up. Then I asked each child questions like, "Where is the animal that likes bananas?" or, "Who is looking out the window?" Then the kids had to locate the correct card and jump on it with both feet, and answer the question. The first time we played this Spencer was concerned that we might wrinkle and ruin the cards. It was an interesting wake-up call to me about how much I have loosened up! Flash cards are just as effective dog-eared and wrinkled as they are pristine and new. The kids loved the game; they even requested it.

I had to learn to relax and not get upset if my goals get sidetracked for a minute, or if it takes longer to get through an objective because the boys are taking turns too. In the end, I think it has been beneficial to Sydney to learn to take turns and to have her brothers involved. It also singles her out less and makes us all feel like part of the group. It helped a lot to move from the very structured ABA based therapy to more natural-feeling play-based and relationship-based therapies.

One advantage that came from including Sydney's brothers in her therapy was that she was forced into learning to work in a group. It is not uncommon for a child with autism to learn "helplessness." Sydney will do as little as possible. When we work one-on-one with her too much, she starts to depend too strongly on the prompts and encouragement that are too easy to offer. For instance, when she was working on her homework and I was sitting next to her at the table, she started waiting for me to tell her if she was right or wrong before she would write down the answer. I had to back off and let her figure things out herself—even if it meant it took much longer and she had to go back and fix things afterwards.

At the beginning of second grade, it took hours to get her homework done when I let her have the independence to do it herself. It was only 10 or 15 minutes of work—and it was not too hard for her. The challenge for her was staying on task. It takes great skill to find the balance between providing her the support to get the work done, and teaching her to do it herself. With her brothers working with us, it was easier to find that balance because she had peers to model, and she had social pressure to keep participating, but there was just enough chaos that I was forced into giving her the independence to learn to do things herself.

Another blessing that came from including her brothers was that they learned to read very young. Isaac started kindergarten reading close to a first grade level and doing second grade level math. Someone at church asked me what I did to teach my boys to read so young. I was confused. I didn't do anything. They learned as they participated in and overheard our work with Sydney.

Most of the time, I feel that because of the way we have chosen to approach Sydney's therapy, overall it has strengthened my relationships with my sons more than it stresses them.

Having a child with special needs can scare a couple into limiting their family size. Special needs kids take extra time, attention, and resources. Especially when genetics are a factor, it can seem very daunting to voluntarily expose yourself to the same challenges with another child. Even if other siblings are born without disability, it can feel as though they might detract from the time and energy needed for therapy, and that in return they can be cheated because of the time the "needy" sibling demands. While we experienced those feelings, especially during the challenging times, we always came to the realization that the real problem was with us and how we were approaching Sydney's autism and the dynamics of our family. Anytime we make an effort to really evaluate what happens in our home, overwhelmingly we can see that our children are a blessing to each other, and a substantial gift to us. While another child with autism sounds exhausting, on my good days I can say, "Why not us? After all, we know what to do now!"

Retrospectively, it was a blessing that I was already pregnant with Isaac when we found out about Sydney's autism. I was so overwhelmed and frightened; I might have put off having another baby. What a tragedy that would have been! We would have missed out on so much; and we would not have been doing what was best for Sydney or for us as a family by waiting; Isaac and Spencer have been good for Sydney, and she is good for them. Sydney has needed her brothers as much as she has needed us, and God knew that and had it worked out in advance. Spencer summed it up nicely one day when he told me, "The best day of my life was the day Isaac was born." I couldn't agree more. So far, the best days of our life were the days Spencer, Sydney, Isaac and later Samuel and Anna were born.

There have been thousands of ways that we have been blessed. It would be impossible to include them all here. From God sending us to Texas, to therapy toy acquisition, to the hidden blessings of graduate school poverty, to the sweet blessing of our children in our home, God has very carefully prepared the way for us to be successful and happy on our adventure with Sydney's autism. Our blessings far outweigh our trials anyway you look at it.

Gift 3: Learning to Love

Learning to Love Brian

When Sydney was diagnosed with autism I became angry. I couldn't be angry with Sydney; she was a baby. I couldn't be angry with the doctors; they were just the messengers. My anger was transmitted to other unrelated events and experiences. Mostly I was angry with my husband. Suddenly, he could do nothing right. He was never home, and when he was, his help was not adequate. He had not done the reading I had, and I was upset and annoyed that he did not know the things I did about autism. He was not learning about autism as fast as I was (based on the fact that he was in a residency program that had him away from home 12-14 hours in a day). I was upset that he didn't know what the therapy goals were and that he couldn't understand what needed to happen. I think I was upset that he couldn't fix it.

I pushed him away and criticized him silently and not so silently. Our relationship was dying, and I was killing it. One day out of the blue I got a call from Sydney's speech therapist. She didn't call to talk about speech therapy. She was calling to talk about marriage therapy. She told me that I needed to know that 80% of special needs kids have divorced parents, and that in the midst of all the stress I had to make my marriage a priority. She told me to call a babysitter, go out on a date, and make a rule that we couldn't talk about autism for one evening.

I don't know if she makes that call to all her clients or not. She was not judgmental or critical at all, but her phone call came as a reprimand, loud and clear. Her phone call changed me. When Brian came home from work I was a new woman. I met him at the door with a kiss and a hug and an "I am so glad you are home." He had the most surprised look on his face. I hung on his shoulders there in the hallway and told him how sorry I was that I had been nasty to him for so long. The kids were clamoring at our feet and the baby was fussing from the bedroom, but I ignored it and told him how much I loved him, and would he please forgive me. He laughed and told me that he knew all along my nastiness was all about having a new baby, my body was not in "reproductive mode" again yet, and my anger was mostly hormonal. I laughed and we had a good long kiss, and suddenly it was not just *me*, it was *us* against this thing called autism.

I think all couples have to make that discovery in their marriages, that you can't let the other demands in life cloud your relationship with your spouse. I didn't learn that lesson perfectly, but it takes me less time to learn it again, and I repent faster. We laugh about the fact that we can become autistic in our relationship. Romantic relationships are very complicated social interactions. When there are too many distractions, we can get hung up on the little nuisances and miss the big picture.

One of the therapy techniques we use for Sydney comes with the warning that you should never attempt to do it if you are tired, depressed, or angry. (You moms out there are laughing your heads off, I know—when was the last time you didn't feel tired?) The entire point of the therapy is to teach enjoyment in relationships. There is a lot about grown-up relationships we have learned from autism therapy. For instance, will we engage in an activity others enjoy, even if we do not care for it, just for the sake of enjoying the other people? Or are we autistic in our relationships where the activity is more important than the people involved? Do we think about how others are feeling and perceiving our interactions, or are our own feelings and needs all-important, drowning out our ability to see someone else's perspective? Just stepping back and asking myself these hard questions has helped me enjoy my marriage more and appreciate my husband for the contributions he makes.

Sydney's autism forced me into letting my husband be more important. Early on, I was so protective; I was very critical of how he interacted with her. It was not uncommon for him to take the boys and for me to take Sydney. Even though I was the one insisting on the arrangement, I started to resent the fact that he was not more help. I learned that it was up to me to change roles. I had to back off and let him learn how to help her as I did—through trial and error and through information about her autism. Once I was able to do that, I saw what was true all along. He had a unique role to fill for Sydney, and their relationship needed to exist without my refereeing. It did not matter if he did not do it exactly as I did. My interaction with Sydney had become too scripted. It was too rigid. And I was trying to insist that he do the same thing. But she did not need two phony relationships—identical with both her mother and father. She needed a relationship with her mother, and a relationship with her father, and they needed to be unique. It was not my place to script it for them— even if that meant it was at times awkward and struggling. Once I placed in him the confidence he deserved, I took a huge step down that road toward marital harmony.

Early on Brian had to say to me, "It is not babysitting when it is your own kids! I do not babysit my children, I am their father." The only way to really learn how to care for a difficult child is to practice. It is a beautiful thing to me to be able to watch my children interact with their Daddy. He is amazing. Sydney went from resisting her father to seeking him out. One afternoon when Sydney was eight, during a period that had Brian working long hours and very involved in church service, Sydney was jumping on the trampoline and yelling, "Where is my daddy? Daddy comes home?" I laughed and wondered what the neighborhood might be saying about us.

I love leaving my husband with my children. Not because I like being away, but because I like the welcome I get upon my return. Brian is wonderful with the kids, but he is not as practiced as me in juggling the demands for attention from the two boys and the need to *give* attention to Sydney. It is not uncommon for him to meet me at the door with greetings like, "You are so amazing, I love you so much." And "You have the hardest job in the whole world." And "I appreciate you so much; no one can do for us what you do." My personal favorite came when Sydney was about three-and-a-half, "Becky, you might as well just give up on the goal of having a clean house, because it is unrealistic." That last comment came when I had left him on a Saturday morning to run errands, and he tried to do some housekeeping while being in charge of the three kids. Housekeeping, attention to boisterous boys, and therapy are hard to mix.

I still have days when I don't meet Brian at the door, he has to come find me in the middle of a dirty diaper or a tantrum with someone and I give him the "It has been a very long day" look. I learned I can still communicate my frustration and my fear to my husband without blaming or punishing him for it.

Very frequently talking to Sydney was like talking to a wall. It took a lot of discipline and patience to keep it up. Talking to any toddler can be like that, and some days it really made me crazy. On one particularly bad day, I locked the chain on the door and when he came home I talked through the door and told him he couldn't come in unless he promised not to make me repeat myself. He had the presence of mind to say, "What?"

It also worked to fling myself at him as he came in the door, grab him and tell him, "Thank you for coming home, please don't ever leave again!" Immediately he had a litmus test for my day—but he was on my side, it was us against them (the kids). He became my refuge, my escape. He's my best friend and my best therapist. My daughter's autism forced me to improve my marriage and love my husband better.

LEARNING TO SHOW AFFECTION

Children teach you how to love. You do things to make them laugh, and when it works, you'll do it over and over again. What you expect in return is the music of their laughter. Your joy is in their joy. If they do not laugh at the game, if they do not think you are funny, then you stop that particular interaction. Relationships, in general, are like this. Most of the time, we only give to get something in return. It may be a smile, a verbal response, a laugh—but we expect something.

Once when Sydney was two, we were finishing up dinner with a guest and Sydney started screaming at me as though she was hurt. I picked her up and could not figure out what was wrong. I tried to comfort her by pulling her close to me and snuggling her, and she started trying to bite my neck and shoulders. I pushed her away and she screamed and clawed at me to be close, and then bit me again. She was as stiff as a board and we couldn't figure out what could be provoking her. Over and over I tried to pull her close to me, only to be bitten and scratched. Finally I held her away from my body with her screaming at me, and I started yelling at my husband, "What is going on? What is happening?"

Our conventional calming techniques were not working and I was very frightened. We tried swinging her, wrapping her in a blanket, putting her down, and even holding her tightly facing away from us. We finally got the screaming and biting to stop and she clung to my neck and wouldn't let go, hiccupping and trembling from her screaming. I carried her upstairs and put her on our bed, then I laid down on the bed in the dark crying. My little girl was clutched at my chest, her tiny person wrapped in my arms, her soft hair wet with my tears. She was so close—yet so far from me. I wanted so badly to release her from her world of confusion and distress and bring her into our world. I was tired of having Sydney trapped and isolated; I wanted to know her thoughts, to know how she felt about her world, to know what made her cry.

I started to pray. I pled with God to help us reach our tiny daughter. I begged for patience and begged for understanding. While I prayed, I looked at my sleeping daughter. Even in the dark I could see the outline of her perfect little ears. I could see her nose, her soft blond eyelashes, her perfectly formed little mouth, and her unflawed, peach-kissed skin. I held her tiny hand—her lacy little fingers were finally relaxed and soft. I started to realize that even with so much that was "wrong," there was even more that was "right" about Sydney. Brian came in and sat on the bed next to us and started stroking my hair. "Becky, I am so sorry." I cried until my head ached and my throat burned, and then I let him take her into her own bed.

Individuals with autism have a very difficult time relating to other people. One hypothesis I have heard is that they are so sensitive to sensory stimulation; it is hard for them to focus on things that are too informative. Human faces and especially human eyes are some of the most information-full things on earth. That is one reason why an individual with autism avoids eye contact—it is very uncomfortable and very over stimulating to have to look at someone's face. Sydney definitely had eye contact problems. As a toddler she couldn't even climb into our laps coming at us forward. She always stopped a few feet in front of us, turned around and backed into our laps—that is how much she wanted to avoid looking at our faces.

Because individuals with autism deal with this over stimulation by blocking out stimulus or avoiding the stimulus all together, they do not learn about subtle social cues and are often socially "backwards" and "awkward." Even with above-average IQ, and the ability to memorize social rules, it still can be a very painful and unsuccessful thing for an individual with autism to learn to relate to other people—and they naturally try to avoid it. Relationships and interactions that are delightful and invigorating to their counterparts are painful and overwhelming to them.

Interaction with a healthy, normally developing infant is very rewarding. For most parents, it is very easy to elicit a laugh from your toddler. Just make a funny face, do something unexpected, play a silly game, or even invite them close to you with your arms open wide and the words, "Come here!" and the child responds with glee and love. Children want to please, want to be close to you, and will interact with you as much as you will let them. In fact, sometimes this constant chatter and the constant wanting the parent to help entertain can be tiresome.

For most of our relationships in life, we only invest where there are worthwhile dividends. We don't pursue friendships with people who treat us with contempt. We learn to take rejection as an excuse to give up on relationships, and unsuccessful attempts at positive social interaction lead to fewer attempts with that person.

Rebekah J. Shumway

For a parent with a child with autism (or a normal teenager for that matter) backing off is not what your child needs. Sydney might be pushing away—she might be running away—she might even be lashing out, biting and scratching. But she needs us to pull her closer, find out what is wrong, and help her fix it.

My mother told me once that you hug your teenage kids even when they pull away and don't want to be hugged, because they need to know that you love them no matter what signals they send to you. I remember stiffening when my mom put her arm around me and acting totally repulsed that she wanted to hug me. But deep inside it was very safe to know that my mother wanted me, even when I didn't want her, and even when I didn't really want myself.

Sydney hated being hugged. I remember the pediatrician who originally suggested we needed her evaluated saying to me, "Babies at that age are normally very snuggly, it is not normal for her to not want you to hold and hug her." We tried a lot of things to help Sydney learn to be comfortable with hugging. Some of the therapy, supervised by our occupational therapist, helped her central nervous system recalibrate to be less sensitive to touch and pressure so she was not as bothered by contact. Some of her therapy consisted of demonstrating that we love her (by doing things that she enjoyed), that people can be fun (by expanding her activities and showing her that slightly new and different things can be really neat) and that hugging is just something that we do when we want to show people we love them (by giving lots of hugs during very happy occasions).

My sister made up a game, the "Big Hug" game. She sat on the floor and put her arms out as wide as they would go, and said, "Give me a BIIIGGG HUUGG!" and then pulled Sydney into a big hug. For some reason Sydney thought this was funny. Soon, she put out her arms too when we said, "Big Hug," and she let us pull her close. Maybe it was because she had warning of our intention, maybe it was because she liked the repetitive nature of the game, and maybe it was because she liked to be squeezed so tightly (it is often much harder for her to tolerate light touch, but deep pressure is not as bothersome.) Whatever the reason—it taught Sydney how to hug, and that hugging was fun. For a long while, if we wanted a hug from Sydney, we had to say, "BIG HUG!" and then be willing to repeat the procedure several times. Initially she did not hug back, but she didn't push us away either. Eventually those little arms wrapped around us, reciprocating the game. She did not squeeze tightly, her upper body strength did not even really enable her to do that, but oh, how good it felt to have her hug us!

The next phase in Sydney learning to "hug," was leaning her head near us when we asked for a hug. She took a step towards us and then leaned her head in our general direction. She carefully kept her feet planted with her body as far from us as possible, but her soft little head extended towards us as a token of affection and acceptance. As we reached out to pull her in, she still pushed away, but we were grateful for the progress.

Sydney's head leaning hug was not unlike the way my big brother greeted me in the halls during high school. I smiled, waved, and gave a verbal greeting, and he grunted and tilted his head in subtle acknowledgement. His greeting did not contain less love than mine—I knew my brother loved me—but he was greeting within the confines of what was socially comfortable to him. After all, what football hero Senior gets all excited and expressive over seeing his kid sister, whom he sees several times a day anyhow?

Sometimes we expect others to love us the way we want to be loved, and we don't appreciate that they do love us. We need to take the time to recognize the ways they show us that love. Sydney taught us to appreciate the small tokens of affection and look for the subtle ways she seeks us out and expresses her affection. At the same time, we strive to teach her how we like to be loved because all relationships need to accommodate other people. We know that in order for her to find social acceptance, friendship, and companionship outside the family, she must learn the give-and-take of normal relationships.

While what I have described was the norm, on very rare and special occasions we got random, enthusiastic, heart-felt hugs. Two arms, wrapped around our necks or legs in brief, wonderful, endearing contact, and then she was off playing again. In fact, once when we had a friend over to play, Sydney kept running up and giving hugs to his mommy. She was hugging so much; it was starting to be a little bit strange. You just never know which way the balance is going to tilt. We have to learn to enjoy the successes, learn to laugh about the idiosyncrasies, and be very creative in our therapy and teaching techniques! Children will learn whatever it is you determine to teach—but you have to learn to enjoy that process and not get too caught up in seeing the end result right in the beginning.

I think it is not an uncommon occurrence for those among us who are the hardest to love to be those who need love the most. Sydney's autism is a challenge in charity. We are forced to learn to love unconditionally. We had to love her, even when it was not apparent that she loved us. We had to talk to her, even if she couldn't answer back. We had to smile and laugh and invite, even when she wouldn't smile back or laugh at us. We had to invite and be rejected, and be undeterred…over and over again. We were transformed by this effort. We loved her more, the more effort we made, and we also recognized how she loved us. We had to learn how to love, even as God loves us.

Learning to Laugh

Often life is so ludicrous, so crazy, and so unpredictable that I have two choices—laugh or cry. I tried the crying method. It was unfulfilling and exhausting. Learning to laugh about things that were previously difficult or even painful was a big step towards finding joy in parenting.

Sydney could recite whole segments of the movie Bambi long before she could put together the sentence, "I want milk." Anytime we went in or out of the front door, she knelt down by the flowerbed and recited, "Eating greens is a special treat, it grows long ears and great big feet." She did this at the park. She did this in others' homes, next to their fake silk flower arrangements. This was funny the first few times she did it. Her recitations were not so funny the 15th or 50th time she did it; then it was just weird. I had to learn to laugh and enjoy the craziness. I try to write down the things that are not funny at the time. Bambi recitation was not funny to me while it was happening. It became funny later.

Once I had regained some composure after Sydney's diagnosis, I tried explaining it to Spencer. He was upset at the turmoil in our house (good and bad) and I was anxious to calm things down for him. Initially, I told him we were taking Sydney to many doctors to help her learn how to talk. He started telling people, "We are trying to get Sydney to talk better. She needs to say things besides just 'cat….' like 'dog'." On several occasions, I tried to explain what all the therapists were going to be doing with Sydney as they came into our home. After one of these conversations, I asked Spencer if he understood what a therapist is. He said, "Yes, it's kind of like cheese." In spite of the serious tone of our conversation, I laughed out loud. I decided to revisit that discussion later.

We have always been baffled by Sydney's love of her car seat as a sleeping arrangement. I know that lots of kids sleep in a car seat as an infant, but Sydney still needed her car seat at the age of four.

Once we started learning about autism and learning about her unique sensory problems, we decided she probably enjoyed the deep pressure she got in the car seat as she pressed her body against the straps. It is not uncommon for individuals with autism to crave pressure.

During the spring right before Sydney turned four, her need for deep pressure increased. For several months (not *winter* months), Sydney needed the security of her moon boots and her snow hat. She slept in them. She wore them to preschool. She wore them to church. Sydney's typical Sunday attire was a long, yellow chiffon-skirted and embroidered dress with accent flowers and bows, tights, her fur-lined purple moon boots and a pink knit snow hat. Sydney was happy as could be to go to church in her boots. I think that six months earlier I would have hated those boots and hat for what they represented, but I had learned that they were an obsession that would pass, and that as her sensory needs were filled she wouldn't need them anymore. My husband and I laughed with friends at church about her "fashion statement."

Not only was she regularly sleeping in her car seat, one night she was crying to wear her boots in the middle of the night. Brian and I started out by saying, "No, it is night time; you don't need your boots on." After listening to the crying for about twenty minutes, I rolled over and said, "Can you think of any reason that we can't just let her wear her boots to bed?" Pretty soon Sydney was in her moon boots and we were all sleeping again. The next morning we knew she was up when we heard the bonk-bonk-bonk of her boots on the hardwood floors.

Sydney's autism helped me realize that sometimes we get into power struggles with our children over things that are just not important, but are very funny. I have learned to pick my battles more carefully. It is challenging to know where the line is between being reasonable with a child and just caving in and giving them whatever they want. My mother told me, "Because you have to say 'no' to a child so often; you need to say 'yes' as much as you can." It has helped me to consider my motivation for telling a child "no." Is it because it isn't a good idea, or is it because it is inconvenient for me? I have learned to say "yes" more often and laugh at the comedy of it.

We had some friends who owned a chinchilla. It was an incredibly soft ball of fluff with ears and a tail. The kids loved to let it loose in the playroom and then chase it under tables and into corners. One day when the chinchilla was out of its cage, Sydney decided to sample its food dish. By the time we noticed, she had almost emptied the entire dish! The dried fruit and vegetables I could understand, but discovering that she ate the green pellet food too was a little disturbing. My friend was really amused. As we were leaving she gave me a baggie of dried carrot shreds to let Sydney eat in the car on the way home. I did not think it was funny until I told my husband, and then because he was able to laugh about it, I found myself smiling too.

Sydney says some very funny things because she memorizes songs, books, movies, and common sayings and then recites them at appropriate or not-so-appropriate times. I recorded a *Sesame Street* episode off the television that had a theme about change. The chorus of a particular song had Sydney enraptured, "Things change, yes they do, both different and new, change can be good too." Several months later, the aid at preschool took her into the bathroom to change her diaper. As they were getting started, Sydney remarked, "Change is good." While the aid was really amused by Sydney's remark, I was saddened by the story. She was simply reciting a line from Sesame Street because of an associated memory with the word "change," she wasn't trying to be clever. However, with a little time and separation from the event, eventually the story became a family inside joke and we use it to lighten up tough moments.

Whether it's sleeping arrangements, clothing, or what she's eating, doing, or saying, learning to laugh at our circumstances has been crucial to finding joy along the journey.

Sydney has had obsessive-compulsive disorder tendencies since she was tiny. This is not really unusual in and of itself, but it makes life very interesting sometimes for us. We work every day at being more flexible and more easy-going about things. Soon after Sydney turned four, we packed two doctor's appointments into the same morning. The appointments were too close together to justify making a trip home between them, but too far apart to go from one directly to the other. So, we bought some gas and drove around for a few minutes to pass some time. Spencer announced he was thirsty right as we pulled up near a McDonald's. I decided that ice cream might sweeten up the entire morning for everyone and give us the 20-minute activity we needed.

Once at the drive through window, I was informed that you couldn't buy ice cream from McDonald's at 8:30 in the morning. Scrambling, I ordered three orange-juices instead. Well, I had already said the "I" word, and a change in the menu meant some major disappointment from the back seat. Isaac and Spencer soon settled for the orange juice, but Sydney started to cry. "Ice cream, ice cream, ice cream." I tried explaining and saving face by making the drive-through teller the villain. "The man said no ice cream!" So, her crying changed to "NO! No ice cream! No ice cream! Man says, no ice cream."

Soon, she was really worked up, screaming, and shaking. I pulled over and helped her take a drink of her orange juice. This changed the screaming to sniffling and crying, "boohoo, no ice cream" take a sip, "no ice cream." I thought we were out of the woods, and started driving to the second appointment. Then the sniffling turned to screaming again, "Oh No! Change a pants! Change a pants!" Apparently she spilled orange juice on her pants. I tried to calm her down verbally, but her screaming became very shrill. I thought that for certain she had wet her pants. I couldn't believe she was that upset over an orange juice spill. I pulled over and discovered that her pants were fine; there was a drop of orange juice the size of a quarter on them. It was too late to go home now for new pants, so we drove on to the pediatrician's.

Sydney continued to scream as I checked in, registered, and paid the co-pay. The toys would not distract her. The secretaries gave me some candy to try; she just screamed between chomps. The embarrassment had me on the verge of tears until I noticed the secretaries laughing in the office, throwing amused glances my way. I sighed and said, "This isn't funny to me today, but maybe it will be tomorrow." They laughed even harder. Finally, after almost an hour of ear-splitting screaming over her pants, she calmed down and was just sniffling about them.

I turned my attention to my boys, and started helping Spencer with a puzzle. Soon there was a tap on my shoulder. An amused elderly woman said, "Excuse me, but I thought you'd like to know that your daughter has taken off her pants." Sure enough, her pants were down around her ankles as she stood at the table playing with a puzzle. Of course, pulling up her pants started the screaming again. Thankfully, the time had come for us to be called back, and we gathered up our things and I drug a shrieking, thrashing Sydney into the doctor's examination room.

When the doctor came in she asked what the problem was, and when I explained she said, "Oh, that is developmentally normal. It even has a name. It is called the 'Princess Syndrome.' Girls this age want to change their clothes twenty times a day for imagined spots and flecks of dirt." I finally laughed. As we left, the office staff all waved and laughed. We went home, changed the now-dry pants, and everything was fine again. Seeing the office staff laugh at Sydney's tantrum helped me summon up the emotional stamina I needed to survive the doctor's appointment without having a breakdown myself. I am so grateful for insightful people along my way who have shown me how to respond with humor to some of the autism insanity.

Laughing changes everything. It helps me maintain perspective on the crisis of the moment and keeps my frustration at bay. It also helps me feel gratitude for what I have, and to recognize the blessings that surround me. Laughing helps me to focus on our progress, and not dwell on things that we cannot change. Sometimes I have to consciously decide to enjoy, not be upset by, those things that are tender. There is always a reason to be upset by the craziness of life. My journal has been a lifeline in helping me to laugh later and reminding me of how far we have come.

Pearls of Love

The Gift of Autism

I haven't always been able to laugh about Sydney's autism. In fact, I have indulged in some impressive self-pity over it. During one challenging period, I was in the "anger" stage of grieving and my soul was hurting. Consumed by our autism problems, I was struggling to function. Out of the blue I had a voice inside say, "Sydney has autism for missionary purposes." I was shocked. That impression had an immediate impact on my perspective of Sydney's autism and the people I met through Sydney.

As a missionary in Hungary, a close friend gave me a pearl necklace as I left the area where she lived. I served in this area for six months, and I had grown to love the people there deeply. This woman was particularly important to me. She told me, "I know after years in the Church that missionaries come and go, and that our paths may not stay intertwined, but we all collect from each other precious pearls of memories, ideas, feelings, and testimonies. Those pearls are always with us, they never go away." I have collected many "pearls" along our journey with Sydney.

Among my favorite blessings from Sydney's autism are the people that we have met through her school and therapy. It has been my experience that only very special people have a desire to work with "special" kids. We have also met some wonderful families who share similar challenges. I have learned some profound lessons in loving through the parent/teacher relationships I have had as Sydney attends school.

Pearls from School

Early on, it was very easy for me to love the people who worked with Sydney. Her therapists and teachers gave her tools to help her find happiness and success in life. Improvement was so obvious. They were like precious gifts to me—these heaven-sent people who could show me how to reach our daughter—how to teach her to talk, to write, to interact, to be happy. But then I had to give up control and send her off to school; preschool first, and then elementary school. No more one-on-one interactions with therapists while I hovered around and participated too. Now she was in a whole herd of children, and I had to trust that what went on while I was gone would be good for her.

Any parent who has ever sent a child to kindergarten can understand my anxiety. I had read so many books that had scared me silly. *You must fight for what your exceptional child needs in school. The system is not set up for children with autism. A bad situation educationally is worse than nothing.* That is what was running through my mind as we went into school. I was terrified that they would be bothered by her. I was afraid they would be so blinded by what she couldn't do that they would not see the great things she could do. My concerns were compounded because Sydney couldn't tell me at the end of the day how things had gone. I felt so protective of her. I felt totally vulnerable to her teachers. I cried through all the meetings as we transitioned her into preschool.

Pre-school was a shock. The shock was—that the teachers were wonderful. They were more patient than me. They thought she was cute even when I did not. They thought she was clever and smart. They could recognize "break-thru" accomplishments that I did not even think to look for. They became my closest allies and very dear friends. I was so grateful for what they did. They nurtured her, loved her and stretched her to help her grow. I remember picking Sydney up after school one day and the occupational therapist ran down the stairs into the lobby with a sketchpad. Sydney had been trying to trace over some simple squiggly lines. The therapist said, "I just have to show you what she did today, look at those gorgeous lines!" It was such a delight to have others rejoice with me in her progress. How do you thank such people? I wanted so badly to do something for them. Money was tight. I decided I would bake bread. I would make jam. I wrote thank you notes. I felt like my "gifts" were silly. And yet, the teachers were grateful. It helped *me* to be able to do something for them. I loved them even more.

Then we moved and Sydney turned 5. Now we were not in preschool, and Sydney was not in a special needs classroom. She was in a regular kindergarten class with 23 other students. I was terrified again. Luckily, I had learned a few lessons. Dress up. Bake bread. These people were going to be *my friends, my allies, and Sydney's hope.*

One of my fears was that Sydney would bother those people who work with her. I know that when I am bothered by someone, everything they do is tainted by my feelings towards them and soon they can do nothing right. Because I know that Sydney might always have some struggles in school, I am anxious that teachers not perceive her as a "problem" to begin with. Because of this fear, I tend to be hyper-concerned about signs that might indicate that a teacher is losing patience with her.

This was my greatest concern with kindergarten. Fortunately, that is not the attitude the teacher and her aide had towards Sydney. They implemented all sorts of strategies to help Sydney be successful in their classroom. The teacher hung a sign on the wall under a table, "Sydney's Spot" it read. Sydney could sneak off and hide under the table when the classroom was becoming too much. She also had a special seat to sit in for circle time; it was very hard to stay in her space when she sat on the floor with the other children. They played to her princess obsession. She had a tiara to wear as an incentive to stay in her seat—if she got out of her seat, she lost her precious tiara.

They also used visual cues and social stories to help communicate to her what their behavior expectation was. She loved kindergarten. She cried on the weekends when it was not a school day. Our school "family" became just that to Sydney—she loved them; we loved them—like family.

It is very easy to love those working with your child when things are going well, but what about when you are not delighted by a therapy or school situation? Every year for us has had its ups and downs. Even in the most ideal settings there were issues that came up in school, and things did not always resolve in the manner I would have liked, or as quickly as I would have preferred. This is just a part of life. The best advice I have been given has proven effective over and over again: You catch more flies with honey than with vinegar.

This attitude change made all the difference for me. I didn't acquire it over night. It took years to figure out—and I am still learning this lesson. It has changed how I feel about Sydney's schooling and about her teachers. It changed how I deal with problems when they arise. It changed how I judge those working with her. It changed how I perceive everyone I meet. This attitude changed me.

By second grade, Sydney had been in three elementary schools in two states. We had worked with over twenty speech therapists and twenty teachers and teacher's aides. Only twice had we been so displeased that we needed to make a staff change. Here is the short list of strategies that have worked for us in happily navigating the early school years:

1.   Be nice.

When Sydney started 2nd grade we started a new school. She was in a self-contained class for most of the day, but part of the day she spent in regular 2nd grade classrooms for reading and math – without an aide. I was anxious for this arrangement to work out, but was also aware of the fact that in a class of dozens of children, it is impossible to give a single child constant one-on-one direction and instruction.

The district used a color change behavior model. If a child was having a behavior problem, his or her color was changed. There were set consequences for each color change. In a previous school, Sydney had to change her color once a week or so. In our new setting, she was getting multiple color changes almost every day— especially in one class. I was concerned that the teacher was too bothered by Sydney for the arrangement to work. I did not want Sydney to feel like a "bad" student, or for other students to label her as a "bad" girl because of her struggles. I did not know if she really was doing that much worse in the 2nd grade, or if the teacher did not understand what behaviors were just products of her autism disorder, or if the teacher was on a shorter fuse, or if the expectation had just been raised. While I wanted the teachers to have high expectations for Sydney, I was concerned that Sydney not be punished for her disability. This can be a hard line to walk. I sent several emails to the teacher asking what we could do at home to help Sydney do better in the classroom. None of them were answered. This, of course, made me worry that she was so bothered by my daughter that she would not even interact with me.

My "Mama Bear" instinct started to kick in. I was frustrated and very upset. Because I could not seem to open up a dialogue with this teacher, I felt cornered and shut out. In an act of desperation I contacted the counselor from the school Sydney attended for the 1st grade and kindergarten. She knew Sydney and me, and working with her had been wonderful. I explained the situation. After listening to me complain she asked, "Have you baked bread yet? You will be surprised at what a loaf of bread will do."

After we left preschool, I had continued to bake bread for all my children's teachers and Sydney's therapists. However, I had not yet taken any bread into our new school. Her message was that I needed to try to open up communication by being a friend, not a foe. I had been too upset about what I perceived as being wrong to thank them for what was right. I took the counselor's advice. I held my tongue and tried another diplomatic route. "Back to School Night" was the next week. I baked bread for my children's teachers. I dropped off the bread and just told them I was grateful for the work they did with my children.

One of the things that Sydney was getting in trouble for in class was biting her hand and humming. I called the occupational therapist assigned to work with Sydney. I explained the situation, and asked her if she had any ideas for strategies we could use to help Sydney. (I will note here that I tried to be careful not to complain about the teacher to the occupational therapist, I simply told her that Sydney was struggling with some sensory problems in this class, that it was disruptive, and what could we do about it? Schools are like small towns—a little gossip can do a lot of harm.) She offered to go do a classroom observation for me.

I also decided to give Sydney's teacher the benefit of the doubt, and assume she had not gotten my emails. So, I printed them off and sent them into school with a note explaining that I had sent these emails, but I was not sure she had received them.

What happened was absolutely amazing. Everything changed. The counselor was right—a loaf of bread makes a big difference. There was warmness in my interactions with Sydney's teachers that had not been there previously. I was so grateful I had not thrown a fit about the unanswered emails. The teacher who was not answering my emails actually had been answering them—but I had never received any of *her* emails. After the occupational therapist observed in the classroom, she reported to me that Sydney was not the only child getting her color changed. She advised me that some teachers are just more prone to change a child's color. Just because she was getting her color changed a lot did not mean that she was being singled out or that things were going poorly. I couldn't compare behavior reports from different teachers in different years.

The bread was a turning point for me. We love those people we serve. Overnight, I was not sending Sydney to a bunch of strangers. These were people who knew I cared about them—and they cared about my daughter. They always had: I just could not see it until I looked for it. Things got better exponentially. I did not use email anymore with this teacher, but instead wrote notes. She made tremendous efforts to keep me informed when issues came up. Our improved communication not only helped me feel better about things, but Sydney also did better. I appreciated the high standards this teacher set for Sydney.

No two teachers are alike. Everyone has a different style. At first I panicked when things were "different." But different does not mean worse. It is hard for everyone to handle change. There is always an adjustment period. But life is all about changes, and in the end it is good for my daughter to learn to be successful in all different types of classrooms. Most people are doing the best they can— especially teachers. I have learned to give the benefit of the doubt and believe that a teacher really is trying to do what is best for my daughter.

Irrespective of how bad it might seem to be going at school, it does not make sense to burn bridges with people who are with your child every day. It is easier to keep a relationship civil and friendly than to try to repair one that has been damaged by angry accusations. All relationships have inertia. Once a relationship is headed in a certain direction, it takes effort to send it in the opposite direction. If I am not happy with the dynamics of one of my children's teachers, it is up to me to make it better.

Plato wrote, "Be kind, for everyone you meet is fighting a hard battle." On so many occasions when something has happened at school that was upsetting, it turned out that I did not have the whole story and things were not really as bad as I thought.

I never regret being nice. It is human nature that others will treat your child better when they have a good relationship with you. I know this from teaching a 7-year-old Sunday school class. The student that drove me crazy was not so difficult when his mother became a close friend. Most teachers love their students even without knowing their parents well. But it never hurts to be nice—it makes school more enjoyable for everyone.

Not every problem will be solved by being nice, but every bad situation will be improved. You can make changes and insist on the things your child needs without ever needing to abandon "nice."

2.   Say "Thank you."

Although I touched on this topic in the "be nice" section, I wanted to address it more completely. My best friend from high school is an elementary school teacher. I knew from her comments to me over the years that parents typically complain when things are bad and are quiet when things are good. The counselor from Sydney's kindergarten school alluded to this too—often parents only get involved when there is a problem. So, an involved parent can scare a teacher into feeling like they are being scrutinized. I resolved to comment on the things that were good about our school situation. It is a good business practice. Employees that feel appreciated and validated are better employees. It is the same in a school environment. I learned I can directly affect the quality of the atmosphere and instruction at the school by saying thank you when things are done well.

The first week of school Sydney was having a very hard time in the car rider line. My sons told me that a kindergarten aide had stepped in and helped her sit with her brothers when she was upset about having to sit separately. I also knew that the school librarian was very involved in the car rider line. So, I sent a note to the aide and thanked her for helping Sydney. I also stopped by to meet the librarian and to ask how things were going with Sydney. I asked if there was something I could do that would help things to go better. She was very gracious and told me that she knew that as Sydney got to know her, things would go better. I sent her an email thanking her for her time and attitude, and thanking her for the work she did in the library. She responded to my email and told me that she had never been thanked for her library work before. How would that be, to work in an elementary school, and never be thanked? I started thinking about all the things that are done for my children every day at school that might be going un-thanked.

This taught me another lesson: Thank everyone. It was easy to send a thank you note in to the teacher that my daughter had every day. Once I started looking deeper into our school experience and thanking everyone, school became a happy place for all of us. I thanked the cafeteria workers for being kind when Sydney started "buying" milk without paying and I went in to pay off her debt. I thanked the school aide who helped her when she had an accident. I thanked the school staff member who was in charge of keeping things under control in the lunch room. I thanked the music teacher for taking the time to put together the school holiday program. When the kids came home talking about a particularly fun Spanish class, I commented to the teacher about it. One night in family prayer my son thanked God that we could go to "such a wonderful school." Our attitudes about school get communicated to our children, whether we talk to them about it directly or not. Thank everyone—from the custodian to the principal. In fact, start with the crankiest school employee you can find—it will make a big difference in your and your child's experience.

At one point when Sydney was having a very hard time in school, in the process of talking to my husband about how to handle it, I kept mentioning that in order to smooth things over with the teacher I would apologize for Sydney's' disruptive behavior. I felt so uneasy about things, I was upset that this teacher perhaps needed me to apologize for things that were, to a great extent, out of Sydney's control. Finally Brian said, "Sydney is a beautiful, darling little girl. Those teachers are lucky to have her in their classes. We do not apologize for her. We do not need to. We thank the teachers for the work they do—but we do not need to apologize for her. She is wonderful."

His insight helped me find peace with Sydney in school. She hums, she talks to herself. She gets out of her seat when she shouldn't. She has a hard time staying on task. Sometimes she refuses to do her work. She drums on the desk. But I do not need to apologize for it. We help her be the best she can. We express the very deep appreciation we feel for those teachers who love her and help her be successful.

3.   Be a team.

The Gift of Autism

My husband and I learned that in parenting you have to present a united front. It is very undermining to a parent and to discipline in general when one parent has a different set of standards than the other. This is true between parents and teachers too. We have found that Sydney makes the greatest progress when we work closely with her teachers and we have the same expectations for her. This means communicating with the teachers and understanding what the expectations are (and agreeing on them), and then doing what we can to reinforce things at home. For instance, we had an incentive system at home for Sydney to reward her when she got her work done at school. Also, if she had a particularly bad day at school, then she didn't get dessert after dinner. I also talked to her about what the behavior expectation was at school, and when there were problems we talked about them at home. We have used dozens of social stories. Occasionally we have had her write apologies to teachers when things have been particularly difficult. We can do a lot to help her school experience be successful.

It has been wonderful when I have had opportunities to help my children's teachers. It is important to my boys that I show up at school regularly. School feels a little safer, and a little less stressful if Mom is there sometimes too. It also helps me feel welcome at a school when I am investing in it. I feel like the teachers and I are working together when I can help them out. It doesn't need to be a big time investment. Make copies, cut out bulletin boards, work on the PTA, help with a holiday party, go on a field trip…or bake bread. Get involved serving by contributing to your school's community.

One day I was walking through the hallway with Sydney when she started announcing to the hallway that she had just watched television all weekend long. A third grade teacher was walking next to us. I said, "Um, we really did not just watch TV all weekend." She laughed and said, "I have been on both sides of the table. I won't believe everything I hear, if you don't believe everything you hear."

Be a team with your teachers.

4.   Understand that nothing is permanent.

Being nice, saying "thank you" and being a team player does not mean you need to sit back and just take it when things are not good for your child. I was so stressed about making our first few IEPs (Individualized Education Plans) exactly right. We agonized over every decision. My favorite school counselor taught me the important lesson that *anything* can be changed. We tried new arrangements all the time. We went from full day kindergarten to half day. We went from pull-out speech therapy to in-class therapy. We changed the class Sydney was supposed to be in based on classroom dynamics right before school started. It gave me confidence to know that we could make decisions based on what seemed to be the best idea, and if it didn't work, we could try something else. This is so important. Sydney's needs change all the time. What works one month may not work the next. This is good. It is a sign of progress and development. I learned to not be afraid to make changes. It is my job to monitor how things are going for Sydney and then advocate for her so things can be as good as possible.

On occasion I have regretted waiting too long to make a change. Now I have a six-week rule. I will try something for 6 weeks. If after 6 weeks Sydney still has not settled in and things have not improved, then I convene a meeting and we talk about how we can tweak things to be better.

I have learned that it is best to not surprise teachers and administrators. As soon as my husband and I are not happy with how something is going, I speak up: "Sydney is really struggling with this arrangement; we are going to do XYZ to see if that helps her. Let's give it a few weeks, and if it isn't better than let's tweak it."

Sometimes things don't work out. Don't be afraid to make changes.

5.   Have realistic expectations.

My favorite teachers are ones who can see the potential in Sydney, and are not afraid to make her reach for it, but are also patient with her when she falls short. At the beginning of kindergarten we sat down with her teacher to talk about some of the issues that had come up. I remember asking Sydney's kindergarten teacher what was *one thing* we could help Sydney master that would go the farthest in improving the classroom experience. She told us that if we could reduce Sydney's self-talk in class it would make a big difference. That became our goal. We focused on one thing at a time. It helped a lot to narrow down our focus instead of obsessing over the huge gap between where we were with Sydney, and where we wanted to be. It was such a treat to work with her kindergarten teacher and see her improve one little step at a time. Sydney never did stop self-talk completely, but she gained more control. Things got a little better. Sydney loved school.

Sydney was a wanderer. In Kindergarten, the teacher learned to put her at the front of the line and hold her hand when walking in the hallway. Then, in the first grade, the teacher put her in line to use the restroom and she wandered off away from her class. The teacher did not realize she was missing for several minutes, and then did not know where she was. The principal found her in the hallway and brought her back to the teacher. I got a note home from the teacher that apologized for losing her at school, but expressed to me that she believed that Sydney was capable of walking in line down the hallway. She was very good humored about the whole thing. She was not upset with Sydney, but rather saw something very specific Sydney could improve. I was so delighted that the teacher believed Sydney was capable of something she had not done before. We wrote a story about walking in line. We practiced walking in line at home. It was not long before Sydney could, indeed, walk in line at school.

A perfect balance for Sydney is a teacher who can be strict with her and set very high standards, and yet is never "bothered" by her behavior when it is less than wonderful. Part of having realistic expectations required me to discipline myself to not be upset when issues arise. One time in the 2nd grade I had to conference with the reading teacher with Sydney because she was yelling during class, "I HATE books!" The teacher and I both frowned and spoke very solemnly about how that is not respectful and not appropriate and plainly not true...and then when Sydney went back into class we shared a laugh and a wink in the hallway. Previously such a problem at school would have been very hard for me emotionally. It was such a relief to be able to laugh about it. I am not in crisis anymore when there are challenges at school.

We had to learn to walk the fine line between making allowances for Sydney to struggle because of her autism, and not letting it turn into an excuse for her to underachieve or misbehave at school. My "knee-jerk" reaction was often to feel as though teachers were almost mean and ignorant—*Sydney can't be quiet, she can't stay in her seat, she can't stay on task without help! How can you expect that from her?* We have learned though, that this line of thinking can be crippling to Sydney and poisonous to us. Now I am so grateful when a teacher sees potential in Sydney and is willing to work with us to help Sydney reach that expectation. We expect great things out of Sydney. When she can't quite do it, we are grateful for teachers who patiently and lovingly help her try again. We improve a little at a time, and then when we think to look back we can see that we have come miles and miles. One step at a time, her autism is a challenge and not an excuse.

Expectations can be a funny thing. It is an important exercise for us to evaluate where our expectations come from. Before Sydney started school, when I was reading about intervention therapies, I used whether or not a child was mainstreamed into a regular classroom as the benchmark for success. It sounds so normal. "My child is in a regular classroom." It sounded to me like, "My child does not have autism anymore." Now I know that mainstreaming is not a reliable measure of a child's social progress. Children can be mainstreamed for the sake of being mainstreamed, unrelated to their skills. I have learned to let go of expectations imposed by comparisons, and instead I want Sydney to be where she can best progress. I want her to listen to her teacher and work independently to get her work done. I want her to have self control over her stimming and her self-talk. I want her to enjoy school. Instead of the mainstream class being the goal, the skills to be successful in a mainstream class are the goals. We are not failing if she needs to be in a self-contained classroom for part of the day. My expectations are specific to her—to what she can do and where she is.

When Sydney was going into kindergarten we moved to a new state. I was very concerned about her school situation and I started gathering information on schools. I narrowed my choices down to two schools—one private and one public. Then I made an appointment to go in and meet someone to talk about placement for Sydney. One school we looked at had been very highly touted as a school that had great experience and success with children with autism. I went in expecting to really like it. I was surprised; the woman I met with asked that I bring Sydney with me, and then she never directly spoke to Sydney the entire time we were together. In fact, her communication to me was "If you get in here, you will be really lucky." And then, "What sort of a problem will your child be for us?"

The next day I went to the public school. I met with the counselor. She spent time while we were together talking to Sydney and to me, making comments and observations about what Sydney could do, and expressing great enthusiasm over Sydney attending her school. As we left Sydney said to me, "Sydney is a smart girl!" Suddenly I did not care what the class size would be. I did not care what the curriculum was. I did not care if the teacher had never seen a child with autism. I wanted my daughter to be in the school where she was wanted.

Give me the teacher who *wants* to work with us. I have tried to reverse that experience and reflect it in my interactions with our teachers. When I go to IEP (Individualized Education Plan) meetings I try to reign in my anxiety and hold off passing judgments. Instead, I communicate that we are excited to work with them and we are determined it is going to be a great year. I ask frequently, "What can *we* do to help make this work?" And I mean it.

The most interesting lesson has been that the person who needed to change the most, in order for school to be a good experience, was not a teacher and was not Sydney—but was I. As I served, wrote thank you notes, looked for the positive, got involved with the intent to support the teachers, and then acted in kindness even when I was frustrated and upset, I changed. I could see more clearly what needed to happen for my daughter. Learning to love her teachers did not make me less observant of what was happening at school, but it did make me less judgmental and more open-minded. I could evaluate better what was effective for her and what was not. When I meet with teachers, I do not need to feel defensive or protective. It is much easier to make decisions and to offer suggestions that will help make things better for everyone. A happy teacher is a good teacher. I am as much interested in the teachers' happiness as in my daughter's—you cannot separate the two and still have success.

Sydney was obsessed with the color pink for years. The first week of kindergarten I put a small pink yogurt in her lunch as a fun back-to-school treat. She was so delighted: I continued to send the pink yogurt. Then one day in the grocery store I noticed small cups of strawberry applesauce. I thought it would be so fun to have a new pink treat. I was so naive. That day there was a big problem at school when she opened her lunch and there was no pink yogurt. The kindergarten aide tried to reason with her about the pretty applesauce...to no avail. It threw off the rest of the day. I got a note home from school about it; "Would you please send pink yogurt tomorrow?"

The-day-the-pink-applesauce-came-to-school lived on as a bleak day in Sydney's memory. In the second grade she was still asking every day before school, "Where is my pink yogurt?" I had to confirm—sometimes multiple times—that she did indeed have a pink yogurt in her school lunch. Every day I send in a yogurt I feel it is a gift for Sydney's teachers. It is one less issue to deal with at school. Her lunch contents are something I can control for them.

On the final day of kindergarten Sydney brought yet another note home from her teacher. This one was not about the sort of day they had. I held it and cried. It simply said, "I will miss pink yogurt."

We had not just survived the school year; we had embraced it—and been humbled by the love and dedication shown to Sydney by her teachers.

Rebekah J. Shumway

The greatest gift this outlook of love has given me is the peace I feel when I send my daughter to school, and the joy I have in the friendships with those who work with her every day. The more I work with them, the more I love them.

So—be nice, say "thank you," look for ways to serve, work with the teachers, make changes when necessary, and be realistic—and then sit back and love elementary school.

PEARLS OF EMPATHY

Before Sydney's diagnosis, I occasionally responded to the Easter Seals mail solicitations with a few dollars. I enjoyed the complimentary address labels, and helping out handicapped kids sounded like a worthy cause. After our experiences with Sydney in Easter Seals, I felt guilty for every envelope I received over the years that I hadn't returned! A grocery store we frequented in Ohio set up a table at the front to sell root beer floats to raise money for Easter Seals. I couldn't walk past without buying a root beer float, and I couldn't approach the table or talk to the employee without choking back tears. Easter Seals therapists helped us turn our frightened, unhappy, non-verbal little girl into a delightful, engaging, sweet little person. Previously, I never knew what Easter Seals really did. Now I know. They give people a chance at life. For a month I cried as I paid $1 for a Sprite float every time I went to the grocery store.

This same grocery store hires individuals to bag groceries who have developmental delays. I have a hard time not crying when I come through their lines. I want to say, "Good for you!" "What a great job you are doing!" But then I think, "They probably want to be treated like they are your average bagger." So instead, I smile and thank them, and comment on the gentle way they handled my fruit. I always think of my mother, who would go out of her way to patronize establishments that hired individuals with MRDD. I don't believe that Sydney's autism has changed the way I treat individuals with similar challenges, but I know it has changed how I feel about them. I want to know how long they practiced with a job coach to understand their job. I want to know about their families and their parents. I want to know about their friends, and what they do for fun in their spare time. I go away from my encounters with them, delighted by their independence in holding a job. I am grateful for programs that will train them, and grocery stores that will hire people like my Sydney. I walk away from Kroger with love in my heart for some manager that I don't even know, and don't even ever see, who is willing to let these wonderful individuals experience the pride and the self-esteem that comes from being employed.

While every disability carries its own set of challenges and frustrations, there is a lot in common between different disabilities in terms of the spectrum of emotions we experience and the way it complicates our lives as families. Anytime I see a family with a child who has a disability, I automatically feel a kinship with them. I feel as though we have common ground, and I love them without even knowing them.

Having a child with special needs changes your perspective on parenting and on other parents. Special needs kids can be very difficult to discipline and keep safe. It takes a lot of creativity to deal with the day-to-day issues. My experiences have taught me to be slow to judge. Unfortunately, it is a matter of fact that sometimes kids with disabilities are abused kids. Child abuse is a terrible, ugly thing. However, I have known several parents who were investigated for child abuse because of ways they were trying to handle situations with their special needs kids.

Rebekah J. Shumway

We have had some scary experiences with Sydney. One night when Sydney was four, she woke up crying and asking to be put in her car seat. When Brian went in to help her, he decided to not fasten the straps to the car seat. That way she could sit in the car seat as long as she wanted, but still be free to crawl out and sleep in her bed. About an hour later I awakened to her cry and I went to investigate. Because he had not fastened her in, she tried to fasten it herself and tangled the straps around her neck and she was choking. When I went back to bed and told Brian what had happened, we were both so upset we couldn't go back to sleep. I lay awake in my bed, haunted by fictitious newspaper headlines; "Child dies when parents strangle her in car seat."

When I hear of situations involving shaken baby syndrome I feel sick inside—not just for the baby, but for the parents too. During some of those times when I have been on a short fuse, when my patience has been stretched as thin as it will go, and I am putting myself in time out and breathing deeply, or locking myself in the bathroom to cry for a minute, I wonder, "How would I handle things if I didn't have the support network I have?" Mentally I start taking away one support at a time. I imagine I don't have a husband, or I don't have supportive extended family. Then I take away my close friends and my church support network. Then I take away my faith and my belief system. Suddenly the stories in the news about parents that snap are about tired, frightened, overwhelmed, sick parents—and not hardened criminals. That doesn't excuse bad decisions and actions, but it does take the hatred out of an already-bad situation. Sydney's autism has helped me love others better and be less judgmental.

My autism pearls are not on a short string, they are ropes and ropes. It is an entire treasure chest of therapy ideas and strategies, of heart-felt conversations, of thoughtful advice and encouragement.

My treasure chest is full of pearls of love. One strand of pearls is memories of love I have felt for those who have worked with Sydney and loved her. Another strand is memories of friends and family who understood and who gave so much of themselves. I have pearls of love from camaraderie when I meet someone who is traveling down a similar pathway. I have pearls of love that I feel for people of which they are not even aware—because they said something that helped, or they accommodated in a way that touched my heart. Sometimes I want to grab my daughter's school teachers or therapists and kiss them—I love them so much!

And then there are times I feel very isolated and alone in the goals I have for Sydney's future. But I am changed by every life that has crossed my path along our autism trek. Some therapists and teachers have remained close friends, even after Sydney is no longer a student. These are treasured friends. I have learned how to love more deeply and with fewer conditions; and I have found more personal joy and satisfaction than I have ever had in my life.

What a tragedy it would be if Sydney did not have autism.

LEARNING татьо LET GO

An important stop for me on my journey of learning to love was a stop at the "loosen up" store. I am not a laid back gal. My parents told me I had to take a stress management class while I was in college as a graduation requirement. I have discovered that sometimes I hold onto pain and disappointment unnecessarily. I am learning to let go of the pain and relax and enjoy the present. I am learning to have faith in God's plan for us, and finding comfort I previously brushed off.

Soon after Isaac's birth, Sydney was having another bout with her insomnia and Spencer was getting up to use the bathroom repeatedly in the night. One night, about the 5th time I was pulled out of bed, I paced in the kitchen for a minute trying to calm down because I was in such a panic about being exhausted and having a new baby and not coping well. I said a prayer and went back to bed and had a dream. In my dream the phone was ringing very faintly. I got up and answered the phone and it was my Mom. She said, "Oh Becky, I am so sorry." The dream ended, I woke up and realized that my Mom wasn't sick on the phone. Her voice was strong and sympathetic. She was okay and she was sorry that I was tired, sorry that I was having a hard time, and sorry that she wasn't there. It was very comforting to me. I was able to let go of some anxiety just from feeling her love.

When I am frightened or hurt, anything can rub me the wrong way. I think it is one of Satan's tools to keep others from being able to help us when we need it. After Sydney's autism I was offended so easily by comments people made or even questions they asked. There was no way to help me because I was "licking my wounds" and was not willing to let go of the anger. God helped me a little at a time to realize what I was doing, and He softened my heart to allow others in.

Sometimes I have to decide to loosen my grip on the disappointment and to open my heart to peace. It's very often a choice. This was a big surprise to me.

Christmas fell about eight months after Sydney was diagnosed with autism. That first year was so intense; we turned our lives upside-down for our little Sydney and she was doing so well! She was talking and able to communicate to us her basic needs and wants; she was enjoying her brothers and wanting to be with us. We headed home for Christmas to see grandparents and hordes of family, and we were excited. I was certain that we would be a "normal" family for Christmas.

We spent a whole month preparing us for it. I wrote picture books for the kids about our trip, complete with photos of both sets of grandparents, the cousins and aunts and uncles who would be there, and the rooms in my Dad's house where we were sleeping. We had a book about the plane ride and picture cards to explain to the kids where we were going and what would happen as we moved between our two families. We packed all the familiar comfort toys and "props" that Sydney might need. My Dad and my Mother-in-law had been very careful selecting Christmas gifts, and I knew Sydney would be getting toys she would just love.

On Christmas morning the kids got up on our Eastern Standard Time schedule (before 5:00 a.m. MST) and we snuck out of my Dad's house and over to my in-laws before the sun was up. Cousins and uncles and aunts and grandparents were waiting for us around a gorgeously lit Christmas tree. My two boys hung shyly in the door to the living room for a minute, and then they crowded in with their cousins to watch the train circle the gifts under the tree and to enthusiastically open any gift that was pulled from the stack. Even Isaac, just ten months old, was right in the middle of the excitement, seemingly unfazed by the jostling, the noise, and the crowd of people.

Sydney refused to come into the family room. She ran up and down the darkened hallway humming to herself. We made several attempts to bring her into the family room or to sit in the archway and just watch—but she pushed us away and went back to her running. A present was pulled from the stack for her. We brought her back into the room and handed it to her, urging her to open it. She let it drop from her hands and strained against our legs to run away. Her brothers came close, excited and clamoring for her to open it. She pushed it all away again. We pulled on the corner of it, enticing her with a peek inside, and still she was uninterested. I held her in my lap while I opened it, took out a wonderful Fisher-Price carriage and with brightly colored horses and little people. She glanced for a moment and I thought she'd take the toys. Instead, she climbed out of my lap and ran back to the hallway.

I was totally devastated. What about all our work? She had been doing so well! She opened other gifts previous to Christmas! She had taken interest in a new toy before! She had been around our noisy, busy families and done just fine. But Christmas was just too much for her. I felt like a total failure, and like my hopes and dreams for her had been beaten to pieces once again. I wasn't dreaming of a college education or a normal life, I was dreaming of one normal Christmas, with the wonder and fun that Christmastime is for young children and their families.

I hung back in the doorway, pretending to smile. I was trying hard not to let it ruin the day. We tucked the other presents for Sydney in a pile next to the sofa, and told everyone we would wait until she was interested. Eventually we let her brothers open them for her. Soon it was my turn to open a gift. My brother-in-law had just returned from Africa on some business. I unwrapped a beautiful black carving of two figures dancing, a mother and child. In a matter of seconds, my heart filled with memories from the last year—the hours and hours knee to knee with Sydney, urging, begging her to communicate with us, the stories and songs, games and toys, the swing, the all-night vigils, Spencer clamoring for attention too—the way he was such a part of all that was happening with Sydney. I thought of little Isaac, sweet and warm, learning at such an amazing speed, laughing at us and still not understanding that his sister was different. I went and hid in the bathroom and cried and cried. My husband came in and I couldn't even tell him what was wrong.

My husband's family was finishing up Christmas, and it was time to go back to my Dad's for their Christmas celebration and brunch. The floodgates had opened, and I cried all the way back to my Dad's. Once there I went and hid in the laundry room—trying to gain my composure. My baby sister found me crying and wanted to know what was wrong. I spilled my heart, told her what had happened, told her about the sculpture, and told her how disappointed I was. She cried with me, and I left her to tend to one of my kids, feeling guilty that I had just ruined her Christmas too.

We ate brunch and then started on the Christmas gifts that were at my Dad's, complete with cousins and aunts and uncles galore. I was surprised at how well Sydney did. It went much better. It was still not my vision of miraculous normalcy, but she was substantially less distressed, and my sisters were careful to pull her in and let her do things at her own pace. Much later in the day I commented to my Dad that Sydney was doing so much better—I wondered out loud why it had been so bad earlier. My little sister commented, "After we talked in the laundry room, I went upstairs to my room and prayed that Sydney would do better, because you were so upset."

I was leveled. I learned so many lessons from that experience! The first lesson was actually just a re-learn—I learned again how much God loves us and how He is concerned with the every-day desires of our hearts. I also learned that my focus was wrong. My sister wisely chose to pray *for me*. It hadn't upset my in-laws that Sydney wasn't participating in the family Christmas celebration. My husband, Spencer, and Isaac weren't upset. Even Sydney wasn't upset that she missed out on opening presents. Sydney's autism was upsetting to me that day because I had an expectation that was not met.

I learned that getting upset doesn't help. Sydney's autism shouldn't be about me—it should be about Sydney, and all we do should be about helping Sydney to have the happiest, healthiest life she possibly can. Now, "happy" does not mean "let Sydney do whatever she pleases," that won't make Sydney happy in the long run. That will stifle her growth and prevent her from having opportunities later. But I needed to learn that "happy" may not mean "like everybody else," especially right now.

Ten months after that Christmas experience, at Spencer's birthday party, Sydney was unwrapping the gifts faster than her brother could "Ooh" and "Ahh" over them. She would unwrap a present, hold it up and say, "Wow! Present for-a-Spencer!" He was a wonderful sport about letting her in on the fun. I remembered what had happened just ten months earlier, and said a prayer of gratitude that we had progressed that far. After that Christmas, I will always be thrilled inside when a child is excited to open a gift.

I can't see that carving from my brother-in-law without remembering that Christmas, without remembering how much it hurt, and without being grateful for the miracle that took place and the miracles that have taken place since then that have changed our Sydney and changed us as her parents. It is a reminder to me that this is a dance—not a fight. We work as partners, one leading, and one following. The music changes and the moves change and the degree of difficulty changes, but it is still a dance. Each day with my beautiful children is a precious gift, and many of our most beautiful, intricate dance-steps we learned from autism.

We have learned so much about love through our daughter's autism. We know more about loving each other, loving new friends, and loving perfect strangers. In the Bible we are told that God is love, so it isn't a stretch to say we've learned more about God through this process too.

Rebekah J. Shumway

Gift 4: The Joy of Discovery

Through this adventure with Sydney I learned to appreciate the miracle of human development. We sat behind a small family in church who had a very young baby—maybe only a few weeks old. His dad held him in his lap, face up, looking at him. The dad cooed and whispered and smiled, and the baby broke out in the biggest grin! His dark eyes were fixed on his dad's eyes—waiting with rapt anticipation for the next smile, the next interaction. I was amazed at the connection and delighted with the baby. I can't help but think in those moments, "Phew, that child doesn't have autism disorder!" I want to tap the shoulder of the parent and say, "Look at what your baby is doing! That is so wonderful! Do you know that is an indication of very healthy brain development, and that is a complicated social interaction?" My husband is probably grateful that I don't do that.

Any parent who has a child with a developmental delay knows that it takes a lot longer for our kids to reach developmental milestones. In fact, we can start feeling like milestones are really "light-year stones," and even wonder if those commonplace accomplishments for other children will always be out-of-reach for our little ones. Autism has taught us so much about human development. Until there were things that were wrong with Sydney, I didn't notice all the things that were *right* about Spencer and Isaac. A human being is an amazing, intricate, miraculous thing. Human intellect, human relationships, human emotions and how we express them, human problem solving, even human physical development—it is awesome and beautiful and amazing. Children learn so many complex skills from seemingly simple tasks. They learn complexities of language—not from lectures and books—but from everyday experience.

For example, who teaches a child to use a possessive "s"? My one-year-old son used correctly and understood that "Mommy's" means "This belongs to Mommy." No one ever explained that to him—he just figured it out by listening and watching. What about pronouns? If you have never tried to think up games to show a child the intricacies of personal pronouns (me, mine, you, yours, his, hers, he, she, they, I) then I think it is hard to really appreciate how amazing it is for a young child to use those words correctly.

We are always trying to take natural interests of Sydney's and use them to teach her skills and encourage speech. Sydney developed a fascination with eyebrows. In my family with a Lebanese heritage, we know eyebrows. Even my blond little babies have full, unruly, bushy eyebrows. She loved rubbing her own eyebrows and anyone else's eyebrows opposite the direction of the hair growth. I decided to capitalize on this and use it to teach her "mine" and "yours." For awhile, Sydney pointed at my eye brows and said, "Mine!" If you think about it, this is very confusing. She pointed at my eyebrows and said, "mine," and I say, "No, they are mine." Then I pointed at hers and said, "Yours." So, she thought her own were "yours." It does not take long to begin to feel like you are playing out the script of a slap-stick comedy.

Sydney's own lack of ability to read social cues has magnified to me her brother's ability to be sensitive to those cues. Spencer noticed that I become very agitated when she wanted to rub my eyebrows so he often said to her, "Sydney, you can rub my eyebrows if you want to." He would stand there stoically while she gleefully rubbed his eyebrows back and forth. Previously, my sisters and I were hard-pressed to muster up feelings of joy over our bushy eyebrows. Sydney loves eyebrows. Her fascination made me stop and notice a dumb little thing like eyebrows.

The more I learn about Sydney's autism, the more I appreciate the little steps she makes towards growth and learning. The more I learn about her autism, the more her brothers' accomplishments and growth inspire and amaze me.

I think every parent is delighted when a child learns something new. I remember when Spencer was first learning to write his name. For an avid reader and writer, there is something so thrilling about seeing a child learn to form the letters of the alphabet.

Sydney had a difficult time holding a crayon correctly. We worked on circles and lines, and worked on making crosses on those lines. Previously, I never appreciated that one day, Spencer could just write out the letters in his name. Sydney had trouble getting her little hands to control the crayon to copy a pattern. She had a hard time processing the shape to be a pattern. It takes upper body strength and posture to sit upright and manipulate your arms in front of you. It takes fine motor control to hold a crayon, keep your fingers around it, and then move your fingers, wrist and arms to move the crayon where you want on the page. You have to move in three dimensions—pressing down and moving in a two-dimensional matrix. It requires visual spatial processing to see a shape and then create it yourself. There is so much that must come together in order for a child to write.

With Sydney, we had to back up to make up steps that other kids whiz over. We worked for a long time to get Sydney to hold a crayon correctly; she wanted to tuck her thumb into her fist while writing. The occupational therapist sent me a paper describing the progression of how a child should develop an appropriate finger grasp. Sydney was still on the "first" elementary hand grasp.

One day we were at the table, practicing with our crayons. Spencer, Isaac, and Sydney had filled paper after paper of pictures, scribbles, circles, lines, and crosses. Spencer was writing his name, drawing cars and planes. I looked down and noticed that Isaac was holding a pencil in a "third" hand grasp. At 18 months old, he was two stages beyond Sydney in how to hold a crayon. Who taught him that? No one. His mind was figuring out through trial and error that he would have the most stability, the most control, if he held a crayon a certain way. I had to coach, trick and encourage Sydney to keep her thumb out of her fist. She wanted to write her name so badly. She begged for us to help her write her name, and she'd say the letters herself as we wrote them. I hadn't realized how often we did that, until Isaac, not yet two, was walking around one day spelling, "S-Y-D-N-E-Y."

One day, I was feeling discouraged and wondering if Sydney would be 15 and still tucking her thumb into her fist. I walked through the kitchen and bent over to pick up an envelope that had fallen off the counter onto the floor. I noticed Sydney had gotten a hold of it and had scribbled on it. As I placed it down on the counter, I could see in tall, distorted letters, "S-Y-D-N-E-Y." Sydney's precious name, written very carefully, by Sydney herself, when no one was coaching and no one was looking. It was as though she said to me, "Come on Mom, you know I can do this. Just have a little patience with me. Look what I *can* do."

Because Sydney did not laugh or smile very often, we pulled out the video recorder and the camera anytime she did. If she thought something was funny, then it was all right to do. We have video footage of Spencer sitting in a ball pit with Sydney. Spencer put a ball in his mouth and then bit into it to pop it out. In the video, you hear me say, "Oh no Spencer, that's yucky." But I am interrupted by Sydney laughing hysterically. She thought that was so funny. I say, "Oh, Sydney thought that was funny!" Which Spencer knew, even at two, meant, "Go ahead and do that as much as you want." We have several more minutes' footage of Spencer biting these plastic balls—popping them back into their laps. We have learned to stop and enjoy the happy minutes. We have learned that even if it is messy or icky or noisy or whatever—as long as it is not *too* dangerous—if it helps us enjoy each other then it is worth doing, and it is worth stopping the rush of life to *enjoy* it. Now more frequently than before, I will stand back and be absolutely delighted by my children.

One magical day at the park, the children discovered the microphone cones that project your voice to the reciprocal cone mounted on the other side of the play set. I stood and watched Sydney and Isaac, hanging on one cone, with Spencer at the other, all three of them laughing and laughing to hear each other say "garbage," "trash," "skunk cabbage," and "Silly Sally." What a joy to see them play together. What a treat to know Sydney understood those words, could say them back, and she knew they were silly.

Autism taught me about play, and about not getting upset about toys under our feet and all over the house. For a while, when I was having a bad day I would throw therapy out the window and spend the day cleaning instead. One day, Brian came home from work to a pure disaster. He couldn't even get in the door because the kids were lined up on their bikes in the entryway, ready to race down the hall. When he came in, I apologized for the mess and the chaos. He said, "I love to see a mess when I come home! That means it has been a good therapy day."

The Gift of Autism

Autism has changed forever how I parent. I have had to realign my priorities and rediscover what is truly important. I have had to force myself to relax, not get too uptight about the small stuff in life, and how others perceive me. On a cold February day at the zoo, Sydney was running behind her older brother up a boardwalk to see the lions. Spontaneously, she turned around and decided to "crab walk" up the board walk instead. Crab walking is something we encourage a lot on the clean, soft carpet at home. It builds great upper body strength and coordination and forces her to open up her palms. With a lot of coaxing and cheering, Sydney will do it for a minute, and then tire and loose interest well before her brothers do.

So, here we were, in all the grime of winter, at the zoo, with Sydney in her pale pink coat, crab walking up the dirty boardwalk. My first instinct was to say, "Oh, yucky, dirty; stand up Sydney!" But instead, I watched her drag her pink little bottom up the filthy boardwalk. I kept thinking about the Canadian geese that overtake the zoo, and hoped that there was nothing deposited in our path up the ramp. Some people came up the ramp beside us, and watched Sydney scooting through the mud. I am certain they wondered what type of mom would allow a child to wallow in that kind of filth. Well now, this mom will!

There are some advantages to living in a home with a child with autism. At our house, we did all sorts of things that are forbidden in other homes. Before we had a trampoline we had a jumping bed—a mattress on some box springs that was fair game for jumping and crashing. We had a swing in our hallway upstairs. When you entered our home, the first things you noticed were the huge slide, mini trampoline, the large exercise balls, and the train table in the front room. Our dining room walls had shelves with toys. You might have tripped on the sit-and-spin in the hallway, and there was no way to miss the "art" all over the back patio windows. We regularly slid down the banister, and climbed up the curving staircase on the outside of the railing. I have had more than one person come into our home and say, "This is kid heaven!"

Not long after Sydney's diagnosis, we awoke one morning to terrible banging from the kid's room followed by laughter. We peaked in on them and saw that Spencer (age 3) was tackling Sydney in her crib. He was not supposed to get into her crib and was not supposed to tackle her, but they were both having such a good time, and we were so excited to see them play together, we decided to pretend that we hadn't seen the infraction. A few minutes later, we heard Sydney cry and we had to go in and discipline. I said, "Spencer, does Sydney like to be tackled like that?" (The normal response to this question was, "no.") He paused and thought for a moment and then looked at me with happy, big eyes and said, "Well, three times she did!"

There is great joy in even small progress. Before Sydney's autism, I never appreciated the creativity that goes into children's play. I remember the first time I saw Sydney pretend a stuffed animal was real. It was naptime, she was strapped in her car seat, and I peaked in through the crack in the door and saw her give her stuffed pig a drink from her sippy cup. I stood at the door and cried. I was so thrilled.

Similarly, it was a treat to watch Sydney take an interest in what her brothers were doing. We got excited when she copied their behavior—even if it was naughty! She went through a phase during which she thought it was really funny to run away from me in the parking lot of the apartment complex. She learned this from her 18-month old brother, who thought it was funny to run away anytime I suggested I needed to change his diaper. Running away in a parking lot is not funny, but it was really hard to get angry with her when she ran away, laughing her head off, looking over her shoulder to see me run up behind her. I was delighted she wanted to tease me like that.

We worked for months and months to teach Sydney to comment about things to try to simulate conversation. One day, while I was trying to keep her brothers entertained in a tiny observation room during speech therapy, her speech therapist asked her if she'd like to blow some bubbles and Sydney said, "I like bubbles." Suddenly, my whole morning transformed, I wanted to stand on my chair and shout "Hurray!" Sydney had commented on an activity, totally unprompted.

Sydney was in kindergarten the first time she told a lie. In the car I asked her what color her behavior card was. She told me it was green. When we got home I started to open the backpack to look at her folder. She panicked and started saying to me, "Oh no! I want to write my spelling words!" She was not on green. She was on yellow for refusing to write some spelling words. I couldn't wait to tell my husband—Sydney had the social awareness to tell a lie.

Potty training Sydney took over a year. Once she got it, she was determined to be independent about it. Soon, I had to listen to hear her open the bathroom door to go inside, she didn't come find me to tell me she had to go to the potty. One day I found her in the bathroom with feces smeared everywhere; it was on the base of the toilet, on the toilet seat, on the floor, and all over her. She tried to wipe herself, and she had a string of toilet paper from the roll, stuck to her bottom, and then into the toilet. In a previous lifetime, I would have been upset about the mess; instead, I was delighted that she did it herself! And she even remembered to wipe!

Part of my journey of discovery has been learning to see the cup half full. I have learned to appreciate the good in what is happening and downplay the negative. Soon after Sydney's diagnosis, Spencer could sense that something was not right at home. Once therapists started coming into our home, it was even harder. Why did these new people only want to play with Sydney? One time of many, when I was trying to impress upon him that Sydney needed help that these people could give, I said, "Spencer, Sydney is having a hard time learning how to talk. These people are all coming into our home to help us teach Sydney how to talk." He was quiet for a minute, and then with those big, blue, sincere eyes fixed on mine said, "But Mommy, Sydney can sing."

He was right, Sydney could sing. Sydney loved singing, and she could carry a recognizable tune with word approximations long before she had any useful vocabulary. Before Spencer said, "Sydney can sing," it had never occurred to me like that. Sydney *can* sing! She is so cute when she sings! What a gift that she can sing, and that she loves music like that.

For a while in her preschool class, her teachers sang any instructions they wanted her to follow. They made up words to familiar tunes based on whatever was happening. She could follow the singing instructions ten times better than spoken ones. I know we provided some substantial entertainment at church to the people in the pews around us when Sydney started singing to the tune "Good Night Ladies," "Sit on the potty Sydney, sit on the potty Sydney, sit on the potty Sydney, it's time to sit on the potty." I was hyper focused on what Sydney could *not* do; my three-year-old could see very clearly what she *could* do.

Working to help Sydney learn to talk one little step at a time has helped us enjoy the normal speech acquisition of our boys more. It is such a joy to hear them talk! I love listening to my toddlers try out new things in their speech. It is amazing to hear complex sentences before they can even enunciate words correctly. I am tickled anytime they respond to a voice command. It is such a thrill to hear them tell us stories and ask questions about the day. I melt anytime I hear a child call, "Mommy, wheh ahh you?" We have learned to discover more about our children and to notice the things they learn. Human development is amazing. A baby is precious. A person is divine. Life to a child is full every minute. Our task is to notice the fullness and discover the joy with them.

Rebekah J. Shumway

GIFT 5: A LIFE'S EDUCATION

Our journey into the world of being a family with autism began when the pediatrician who diagnosed Sydney gave me a reading list of recommended books. Autism is not like cancer or a bacterial infection. For most parents who discover something is "wrong," the doctor says, "Something is wrong, this is what it is.... this is what I think we should do." For a child with autism, it is rare for the diagnosing pediatrician to also recommend treatment. So, it feels a whole lot like they say to you, "Something is wrong, your child has a neurological disorder that will affect them the rest of his or her life, but with intense therapy things may improve. Good luck to you." We heard a lot about early and intensive intervention. What in the world does that mean?

Back in the 70's my parents had some friends who built a home for themselves from a kit they ordered. A semi truck came, dropped off piles of building supplies, and then drove away. I remember my father's friend relating that it was the loneliest feeling in the world to watch that semi drive away, knowing that the pile of building materials had to be turned into a house, by him. This is a pretty good description of how we felt about beginning therapy with Sydney. We felt very lonely, overwhelmed, and uncertain.

For years, there was not much available to individuals with autism and their families. They were declared profoundly retarded and many were taken from their families and institutionalized. For many, behavioral problems stood in the way of making cognitive and social gains that we now know are possible. Because the system was not set up to understand or help these people, many were mismanaged or not managed at all. When I first started reading about autism and even speaking with parents of autistic children and adults, there was a very strong undertone of distrust and even disdain for people in the field of traditional special education. This is very disturbing and very upsetting to be told that the "specialists" in an area are not special enough to help you! It drove me to read all I could, to find out all I could, to know as much as I could about autism, and what our options were for our little girl.

I took the reading list the doctor gave me and went right to our local library website. Of the thirty books on the list, three were in the library system for the entire city of San Antonio, Texas. Two of those books were children's books, written to help siblings of individuals with autism or to help other children understand a little about autism. So, I went on an Internet shopping spree. $400 was just my starting amount. Books started arriving, and I started reading.

My husband teased me that I was working on a graduate degree in autism. He was right. I did the background research on a problem or a therapy method. I evaluated the pros and cons. I formed a hypothesis about how/if it would help our current therapy situation, and then we applied it, testing our hypothesis in our home laboratory. I kept copious notes and tallied our progress. My experience, my reading, my association with other therapists and teachers, conferences and workshops—it all came together and made the first few years after Sydney's diagnosis an intense learning experience for me.

God not only positioned us in Texas with people we would need for support and example, but we were also well positioned to begin our autism education. In the months that followed, there were two conferences on autism held in San Antonio. One was for parents with a recently diagnosed child and one was on a particular type of therapy. Both conferences were instrumental in putting us on the right therapy track for Sydney. They also established a habit for me of attending such conferences. I have never left a conference without feeling like I received valuable information. Once we were back in Ohio, I attended one conference that convinced me that a certain popular therapy was *not* right for our daughter—but even that was valuable because we didn't waste time, energy and money pursuing it.

In some ways, I know autism better than I know chemical engineering. I have had to apply every bit of my knowledge as I go. There is no degree awarded at the end of my program. In fact, there is no graduation ceremony or even a graduation date. My grades are posted when a new problem arises and I am challenged to find a solution to it. The diploma comes when we have truly mastered a skill and I stand back in delight and watch Sydney use a part of speech correctly, un-prompted, with a new person. My homework is due every day as I try to come up with new and interesting ways to teach a skill.

Multitasking was taken to a whole new level as I tried to juggle therapy goals into everyday play that was developmentally appropriate for my daughter, and would still involve her brothers. Between therapy sessions I also had to make meals, manage our finances, and keep the house clean enough to not be in violation of health code.

In all the reading I have done, all the conferences and lectures I have attended, and all the thousands of hours I have clocked experiencing autism, I have learned that I do not know very much about autism. My personal experience with therapists and teachers has been that every one of them has given me something unique. They have all been helpful. Some, certainly, are more helpful than others, but there is no way we could have provided what our daughter needed without the help of dozens of other people who have had years and years of training, experience and education.

The symbol for autism is a ribbon made up of brightly colored puzzle pieces. That is exactly what it is like. I gather pieces to a puzzle from hundreds of different people, none of whom have all the pieces, and then try to shape together answers for our daughter that are individualized to our family that address what she needs and how she should get it, and what our expectations for her should be.

My graduate school of autism has also become a graduate school of parenting. Autism is about developmental delays in key areas of language, social, emotional development, and cognition. My daughter is delayed; meaning her age in years is not reflected in her abilities and her skills. But all the things I learn about autism have helped me relate better to children in general.

Around the time of Sydney's diagnosis, Spencer was getting in trouble frequently for not obeying on demand. I felt like we were fighting all day over the details of existence. Simple requests, like "go get your shoes," or "pick up those race cars and put them in the bucket" were met with blank stares and little action. Because I was upset (about Sydney) and exhausted (new baby), my patience and my nerves were on short fuses and there was a lot of conflict during the day. I felt like I was repeating myself constantly—and I was.

During this time, we attended one conference put on by "Any Baby Can" in San Antonio for parents of children with autism. Some special education teachers gave a presentation on effective communication techniques in a classroom. One teacher made the point that typical preschoolers can take up to 15 seconds to process language. She counted out for us 15 seconds so we could feel just how long 15 seconds really is. Her point was that if a normal child can require up to 15 seconds processing a voice command, it is going to take even longer for a child who has auditory processing problems to respond to a request.

    Kids are smart, they memorize what commands mean, and they program themselves to respond, but it takes time for them to process language. I was getting parenting coaching for Spencer, not Sydney. At that time, I couldn't imagine giving Sydney a voice command—she wouldn't even respond to her name being called. Spencer was getting in trouble all day for not responding. Maybe I was just not giving him enough time to process what I was saying. I doubted it; Spencer was very verbal and did not seem to have any trouble understanding or communicating with us. The next day, I decided to test out the teacher's point. When it came time to leave the apartment, I said to my son, "Spencer, get your shoes and come here so I can put them on you." Then I started counting silently in my head, "one, two, three…" he still sat on the floor with his toys, acting like he hadn't heard me. "Four, five, six…" he looked up and kind of studied me as if to say, "Were you talking to me?" "Seven, eight, nine, ten…" he finally got up off the floor, and went to fetch his shoes.

    Previously I would have waited about half a second, and then repeated the request, waited another half-second and then gotten angry. I was so impatient with Spencer when he didn't jump just as soon as I gave him instructions. Spencer used to get put in time out for not coming when I called and not responding when I asked him to do something. I thought he was being lazy or belligerent. Really, he was just processing what I was saying and figuring out what to do.

    Autism taught me to give my kids the benefit of the doubt. I don't think there are very many preschoolers who are belligerently disobedient. They don't do what we tell them because they are busy doing other things, they don't process language as fast as we do, and because they don't always understand what we ask of them. This insight has helped me enjoy my kids more because I am not as frustrated by them. I understand better that what is expected of an adult is unrealistic for a child. Now, I think I have reasonable expectations, and that makes a big difference.

Autism also taught me that there is a "why" behind most behaviors. Kids are not random; I think they are more calculating and more deliberate than adults. A child is not fussy or overly sensitive just to aggravate a parent. I recognize now that tantrumming and mean behavior like hitting and biting can come from being over tired, being hungry, being frightened, or being over stimulated. I have been wrong more than once in assuming a child was being difficult, and then discovered the child was not capable of doing what I asked him or her to do.

As Spencer got older, I grew increasingly frustrated that he couldn't locate items that I sent him to find. He could be standing right on top of his shoes, and when I told him where they were, he just looked around confused. It was a waste of time to ask him to find things, because he never could. I also remember driving in the car and trying to point out something fun to him. I'd say, "Look over there Spencer." In the rearview mirror, I could see him look opposite the direction I was pointing. It was frustrating for both of us. When he was four-and-a-half, we learned that he is severely far sighted. He wasn't lousy at finding things because he was not careful or not diligent—he just couldn't see things.

Sydney went through a stage of visual "stimming," or so we thought. She squinted a lot, looking at lights and windows, and tried to look at things out the corner of her eyes. After her brother's near-sightedness, we took her in and had her eyes checked. Once we got glasses for her, the squinting and the sideways glances stopped entirely. I will admit, I do not know if it was the glasses that solved the problem, or if it was the time it took us to get the glasses. It may have given her time to grow out of that obsession. It took us four trips to three different eyeglass shops and over four months to buy Sydney a pair of glasses that fit and that she would tolerate.

Beginning therapy was like having the sun come out, not just because Sydney started improving, but also because we started learning the reasons behind her strange behavior. That knowledge and understanding made all the difference in our ability to help her and to accept our situation. There is always a reason for a behavior.

Our little Sydney is a toe walker. She dances around on her toes wherever she goes. When she was tiny we thought it was darling. Friends commented on it all the time—our little Prima Donna dancer. Once I started reading about autism and I discovered that the behavior had a name, toe walking, and that it was a common trait among individuals with autism, the toe walking wasn't cute any more. I was sickened when I watched her run on her toes, and it hurt when friends and acquaintances would innocently comment on it. Finally, someone explained to me *why* Sydney toe-walked. An occupational therapist explained that because of her gravitational insecurity (her inability to know where she is in space), she does not rely on her inner ear for information about her balance. She uses her proprioreceptive sense—or her joints instead. So, while the rest of us feel secure with our feel firmly planted on the ground, she feels more secure with her ankle joints in the "closed" position—or up on her toes.

It is helpful to know the why behind autism characteristics. Instead of thinking a behavior is strange and being upset by it, I understand it, and sometimes I know better how to help her overcome it. This perspective has helped me in many other ways. I assume that my children's behavior is deliberate. They are not random creatures. I am slower to anger and pass judgment on strange or "bad" behavior, and quicker to ask, "Now what could be going on that would make that child do that?"

I have overwhelmed friends who have casually mentioned problems with their kids with a list of possible solutions. Several friends mentioned problems with their 2, 3 or 4-year old still mouthing things—I pull out my bag of tricks. They get a list of reasons why their child might be mouthing toys and then suggestions of things they can give their child instead. I pull out vibrating chew toys, straws, bubble blowers, whistles, and kazoos. I tell them to try beef jerky, licorice, Popsicles and frozen fruit.

Some friends are grateful for the suggestions, and some have looked at me as though to say, "Um, thank you, but I think for now we will just tell him to take the toy out of his mouth and wait for him to grow out of it." Before Sydney's autism, I would have been in that second group of parents. Autism has been a graduate school of parenting for me.

Sydney's autism has also been a graduate school of relationships. Autism is a relating-to-others disorder. I have heard many parents of teenagers with autism say, "He is doing well in school, but he just can't make any friends." They are less concerned about reading, math and language skills, and more concerned about the lack of social skills. Typically the employment prospects for individuals with autism are grim. Not because they are not capable of the jobs, and not because they are not intelligent individuals. Unfortunately, a low percentage of even high-functioning people with autism are able to maintain employment. The reason is their inability to relate to people.

Rebekah J. Shumway

Studying the pathology in autism relationships has forced me to reevaluate my own relationships and uncover the pathology within them. It takes constant work to make my relationships with family and friends my top priority. It is very easy to allow routines, convenience, and vanity to take a higher place in my list of priorities. For instance, am I happy to have out-of-town friends come over, even at an inconvenient time, because I am happy to see them? Or, am I so obsessed with my list of chores or the potential embarrassment over my unfolded laundry that I unwittingly make them feel unwelcome?

I think a major pursuit in anyone's life is balance. Learning balance has been a major course in my life's education, a course I have to re-take continuously. Balance between life and work, between family and hobbies, between church and civic obligations, between friends and family—it is hard to find and maintain. Finding balance becomes even more important when one aspect of a person's life is disproportionate with respect to the others.

Balance became very important to me as I divided attention between my little ones. I found that it took a lot more work, but it was more satisfying when I included everyone whenever I could. I learned that we couldn't live in a bubble; we had to go on play dates with friends and attend church parties, even if it meant that Sydney ran around crazy for a few hours. Sometimes life had to be about what was good for me and what was good for the boys or their Dad. It was also very important that we only considered therapies that allowed us to continue to function as a family. This makes such a difference. Sydney is a very important member of our family, but she is not the center of the family. Life should not start and stop for her—I do not think it is healthy if it does.

Part of my life's education has been learning that what goes up, must come down. In much that I have read about autism, people have noted that it seems as though individuals with autism may have windows of normalcy—times when they are very connected with what is going on and they understand and interact with their surroundings in a normal way. Our Sydney has these moments. She has even had periods of several days at a time when she is so aware of us, connected to us, and enjoying her environment. I've had her teachers comment on these days. They want to know, what did we do? Was it something she ate? Was it something we did at home? Is she sleeping better at night? Are we turning a corner? We get very excited when a window opens, but I have learned that they shut—and we have bad days again.

We worked on teaching Sydney pronouns for *several years*. One day, things started to click. She went from talking about herself in the third person, "Sydney's turn," to understanding that she was an "I" and a "she." So, we started hearing a lot of "What is she doing? She is eating." We started pushing her to talk about herself in the first person, "What am I doing? I am eating." It was going very well, and then we had a turn-around, where not only was she only referring to herself in third person, she was a "he."

For months answering yes/no questions was a goal we had for Sydney. Most two-year-olds master "no" very readily. Sydney was four once she got it, and when she did, she routinely yelled, "NO!" anytime she was asked to do something. Not wanting to undo all our hard work, we wrote stories about when it was appropriate to express an opinion, (e.g. "Do you want more milk?") and when it was not (e.g. Time to change activities at preschool). I was discussing this issue with Sydney's preschool teachers and expressing frustration over the fact that it seemed the more we worked, the worse the behavior was getting. They shared a wonderful little nugget of insight; "Every behavior is going to get worse before it gets better." They were so matter-of-fact. They were not concerned at all about her little assertions of four-year-old rebellion. And, they were absolutely right. Everything gets worse before it gets better.

Watching behavior get worse in spite of our efforts used to really upset me. Those times are still disappointing, but I know now that it is a step towards mastering a concept. It is not the end of the world; she had it once, she will have it again, and this next time it might be a skill she retains.

Understanding that she has good and bad days has helped me appreciate the good days more. I am not as inclined to brush her off if she wants to come to me and play—it may not happen tomorrow. This lesson has been helpful with my other kids too. I listen to my 5-year-old's ramblings better—he might not want to talk to me eventually. I put down the dishes to read a story to Isaac—he won't always want to point to everything and show me he can say its name. Those times when Sydney is interacting with us—within her capacity—everything stops and there is nothing else going on in the world, just our little family enjoying one another.

I have learned a lot over the past few years, but we are still new players in this game. We haven't hit puberty, high school or adulthood. We haven't needed social skills classes or job coaching yet. In many ways, we are still in a honeymoon period of Sydney's autism. She is cute, progressing well, loved by many people, and mostly only teased by her brothers. I know that can all change. I am not so naive as to think that there are not challenges ahead of us; in fact, I know the opposite is true. We are on a lifetime journey. My hope is that Sydney never stops learning, and that I never stop learning either.

Gift 6: Celebrating our Uniqueness

Perhaps my favorite gift from the treasure chest of our autism experience is a greater appreciation for the uniqueness of every individual on earth. We live in a society that is comparison obsessed. We are always trying to measure up to some elusive standard of appearance, success, and behavior. We feel that somehow differences must be rated—have some value assigned to them—so things are not just different, they are better or worse.

Very soon after Sydney's diagnosis we were at the church sitting in the foyer with some other people. I sat next to a friend who was there with her little girl who was slightly younger than Sydney. The girl was pointing at us and looking at her mom, smiling, and playing peek-a-boo. I could hardly breathe—I was so jealous and heartbroken. Two weeks before it would not have bothered me—Sydney was Sydney and she had a unique personality. But once that "personality" had a name, it became hard to watch her and hard to watch other children. I was grateful for the arrival of Isaac, because I had an excuse to hide for almost a month. I went a week without answering the phone and a month without seeing most of my friends. I had to get a grip. I compared Sydney to everyone; her brothers, other kids, and even other children with special needs. I lost track of who Sydney *was*, and only could focus on who she was *not*.

My mother tried very hard to teach us to avoid comparisons. Comparisons leave you feeling either superior or inferior—neither of which is a healthy feeling. In Texas I fought to keep the comparison monster at bay. Because I was not emotionally strong, I did it through isolation. We did not associate with kids who were exactly Sydney's age, and I did not ask parents about the ages of their kids. I didn't want to know.

This worked fairly well for me until we had to move back to Ohio. Right after we moved, I had a friend invite us over to play who had been in the hospital having a baby the same day Sydney was born. We shared the same labor and delivery nurse, and this friend and her hours-old baby had been Sydney's first visitors. I was anxious to see her and to renew that association. I was not prepared for how I would feel when I saw her little boy—who was exactly Sydney's age. It was really hard to see him follow directions and talk in complete sentences. I was stunned at how far behind him Sydney seemed. Suddenly, all her amazing progress seemed like nothing in comparison to where she should be. I couldn't help but remember the hospital visit. Our children came to earth on the same day, why did they not have the same abilities?

For a long time I went along in my little bubble and because no one else was *exactly* her age, I pretended that she was normal and that she was doing well. I focused on her progress and felt really good about things. It knocked the wind out my sails to see her peer, and to see that she really has autism. Subconsciously I was still holding out hope that one day I would wake up and the autism would be gone.

Sydney's autism taught me that you have to accept people where they are, and have unique expectations for them. We are going to notice differences between people; it is an important skill to have. Differences are not the problem. The problem is the prejudice that those differences, both good and bad, mean that *someone* is "better" or "more valuable" than someone else.

The Gift of Autism

By three months, Isaac knew more about relationships and communication than Sydney did at two years old. He knew that if we smiled at him, and he smiled back, then we would laugh and talk to him some more. He knew Spencer was always interesting to watch and Isaac would strain to find him in a room when he could hear him. He knew our voices and would respond to our soothing talk. When Spencer was still non-verbal, if he began to tantrum we could say to him, "Spencer, that behavior is not appropriate," and very often it would stop. Like all children, sometimes he was difficult to soothe, but most of the time we could figure out what was wrong, remedy the situation, or reason with him to dissipate his anger and frustration. Sydney didn't understand anything we said, and we didn't know why she would scream and cry for hours. This behavior was certainly different than that of her brothers, and it was certainly less desirable, but it didn't mean that *she* was less desirable. It just meant that we couldn't treat her like we treated her brothers. We had to rewrite our parenting strategy for each child, an important lesson to learn.

My mother used to say that if you raise two children the same, then you are raising at least one of them wrong. The same can be said for children with autism. No two children are alike; they have different needs at different times. I have felt that there is a lot of social pressure in autism networks to give all children with autism the same treatments. There is a lot of comparison that takes place, understandably, because parents are searching for something, anything that will help their children, and traditional medicine often falls painfully short.

Unfortunately, there is a desperation that surrounds all of it. As a parent I wanted to give Sydney anything and everything that would help her overcome autism. I started out determined to cure her. I do not think that I was unique in that respect. All parents want the best for their children. The problem is, what is best is hard to define. I have seen parents jump into popular therapies without much research or investigation, and without a clear understanding of their children's needs. Often, they are looking for answers to a question that has no clear or simple solution. Any case study that reports improvement in a child with autism holds a glimmer of hope for the existence of the holy grail of autism remedies. In my opinion, it is a heart-breaking, very intense example of "keeping up with the Joneses." I have also seen therapists try to apply a certain technique or method without consideration for the developmental level of the child. Not all therapy works all of the time, and for every stage something might work differently.

That was certainly true for Sydney. What was best from a therapy perspective when Sydney was two was not best for her at four. There is no way for me, as a stranger, to tell any parent what would be best for their child with autism. Every child is different and needs change as development happens. Living with Sydney has taught us increased flexibility and made us more sensitive to the unique needs of individuals.

The more you read and learn about autism, the more you can see autism in people around you. Reading the autobiography of an individual with autism is an eye-opening experience. You will be surprised about the things you relate to and those things that are foreign to you in their experiences. In my experience, many autism autobiographies cause the reader to self-diagnose themselves with autism. My husband and I joke, "We are all a little autistic!" This viewpoint has changed how I feel about people in general. It has helped me to be more tolerant of the strangeness in all of us.

Sydney is my girl, and while they haven't yet isolated an autism gene, there is substantial evidence to suggest that it is inherited. Knowing this and then learning about autism has helped me to recognize the autistic tendencies in our families. Even more fascinating is observing these behaviors among friends and colleagues and everywhere I go.

For example, Sydney is tactile defensive. That means that she is very sensitive to touch, and some things that are not bothersome to other people bother her. When the occupational therapist described this concept, I laughed. I know exactly what tactile defensiveness is! I am legendary in my family—and we all hate being touched. I remember my mother telling me that it was very uncomfortable for her to hug us; she hated having someone in her personal space. She was a warm, giving individual, but she was tactile defensive. My dad will only wear long-sleeved dress shirts. I have memories of him standing chest-deep in a lake teaching me to water ski in a long-sleeved, collared dress shirt. He can't stand feeling things rub on his forearms.

Some individuals with autism are very sensitive to light and visual stimulation. Well, there are a lot of fluorescent-light haters out there. I was driven to the point of distraction at work or at school when I had to sit under a flickering fluorescent light. Occasionally I have even talked about the bothersome lights, and been surprised that no one else could see them flicker.

Growing up, my mother made some seat covers for our van, one of which was a blue and white pin striped double-knit polyester. I was always in a foul mood when I had to sit behind the seat with that seat cover, because it made me feel dizzy and motion sick to see the blue lines. It never occurred to me until after Sydney's diagnosis that that was unique to me—I just assumed that everyone hated the striped seat cover.

My sisters and I all are very smell sensitive. I can get physically sick from a smell that is offensive—and it doesn't have to be strong. I can smell a cologne or perfume on a person from across the corridor at the mall. I can smell garlic on my husband days after he has eaten something with a lot of garlic. When I am pregnant my nose is especially overactive. I pick restaurants by walking inside, taking a deep breath, and testing the air. My patient husband has followed me out of more than one eating establishment!

Autism isn't just in my family. I have a brother-in-law who can't sit down to talk. He only rarely makes eye contact and he paces like a caged animal. He can't stay in the room with the rest of the family for more than twenty minutes at a time. There is no way he would be diagnosed clinically as autistic. He just has this little "autistic tendency."

Now that I have called attention to some of the quirkiness in our families, I have to say: our families are not the only ones in the world with autistic traits. What about all the picky eaters out there that have major issues with food texture? What about those people who do not understand appropriate conversational distances, and invade your personal space constantly? What about all the obsessive-compulsive people? What about those friends who just need "alone time" once in awhile? What about the difficult co-workers who seem to have no sense of tact? Are they really unfeeling and mean, or do they just lack the ability to read social cues and lack "theory of mind," or the ability to understand how someone else feels? We all have funny things about us; sometimes the only difference between having autism disorder or not is a matter of the degree of the quirkiness, and the coping mechanisms we may or may not have to deal with the things that bother us.

The Gift of Autism

I have found that I am more generous with people, and I give people more space than I did before Sydney's autism. We all tantrum in different ways, and there is no way to know what a person is feeling and thinking at any given time that might cause a behavior. Brian and I will laugh all the time at idiosyncrasies we see and say, "That is so autistic!" Instead of judging others, I love them for their funniness.

I have learned that life is fullest when we not only accept differences, but we learn to enjoy them as well. We had some friends come for dinner who did not know that Sydney has autism disorder. I noticed that during dinner our friend kept watching Sydney as she sang to herself and spoke in her stream-of-consciousness way. Out of the blue she said, "She is very interesting." She was right. Sydney is very interesting. She recited books, movies, songs, and phrases she'd heard verbatim, but she couldn't answer a "yes/no" question. For a long time it was easy to think that she only spoke nonsense, but if you listened very closely, you could hear her connect to what was going on. It is a lot of work to follow her complicated web of associations, but we are all worth knowing, and we are all worthwhile.

One experience in particular was an intense test in appreciating the gift of our uniqueness. It was a lesson that I did not expect, and it came when I was seeking answers to a different set of questions.

For eight months after Sydney's diagnosis, we followed a very strict, very structured therapy plan. It worked beautifully. She was learning quickly and making wonderful progress. In those eight months she went from zero useful language and almost no communication skills to having a vocabulary of hundreds of words and hundreds of signs, and starting to combine words into phrases. She went from totally non-responsive to verbal direction to a child who could follow simple, familiar commands about 25% of the time. She was more secure in her structured environment, and we had her on a sensory diet under the direction of an occupational therapist. Sydney was a happy, sweet little girl.

Then January happened, and our world fell apart. Sydney started to resist therapy. She screamed and cried and totally refused to cooperate anytime I pulled out familiar flash cards or activities. Skills that she had once been able to perform with ease she seemed to lose, and we were very afraid we were headed into a regression. I was frightened and consumed by what was going on.

Brian and I started praying and fasting that we would know what we needed to do. I told Brian, "We need a new therapy plan, but I don't have time to re-read all those books! I need to know what to do, and I need it to just fall into my lap." That week we got a babysitter and we went to the temple together for the first time in a long time. During the session I did a lot of praying and pondering. As we left the temple, I turned to Brian and asked, "Well, what do you think we should do?" He said, "I think we are really lucky to have her."

His answer surprised me. I wasn't feeling lucky to have her! I mean, of course I loved her, but I was so consumed with the trials of raising her, I had totally forgotten to have any gratitude to just *have* her. I am grateful for that experience at the temple with my husband.

Sydney's autism taught us important life lessons about accepting people where they are and individualizing our expectations. Everyone progresses, but not everyone progresses at the same rate. When I get past comparisons I find great joy in seeing Sydney reach her small goals. When I get past comparing myself to others I find satisfaction in the little accomplishments of the day. We have to start where we are. Each of us is unique; we are individually like a rare and precious gem. There is only one of each of us in all of existence. We are all here to learn and love and grow, and to cherish the other children of God that He allows us to know.

Conclusion

We found new therapies that were better suited for Sydney. After that trip to the temple, I remembered a conversation with our Texas occupational therapist months earlier that prompted me to do some Internet research. That led me to several new books and an entirely new perspective on therapy. We found something more play-based that seemed to fit Sydney's current temperament and our family situation better. That same week, I attended a conference and was impressed by a presentation, and we started implementing some therapy that was more relationship based than skill acquisition based. This also proved to be a right move for our family. The answers to our dilemma did "fall into our laps," and we started making progress again. There will always be more to try; hitting a "brick wall" is just an opportunity to grow our faith and test our resolve.

Since that day in the temple, we have repeated the words "We are lucky to have her" many times. I say them to myself almost daily, not just about Sydney, but also about all of our children. We are lucky to have them. They add spice and meaning to my life in ways I had never imagined. They each add a dynamic to our family that enriches us and brings us great joy. Sydney is no exception. She has a gentle, playful, teasing soul wrapped in a beautiful, small perfect body complete with enchanting dimples and a sweet, melodious voice. She is a little angel here on earth—sometimes seeming out of our reach, but always very close by. We could very easily be envied. We are lucky to have her. It is delightful to get to know her better each day, to open the door between her world and mine and walk though this life together.

The Gift of Autism

We have come a long way from the survivalist panic that we felt in the beginning. We still have moments when we mourn Sydney's autism, but they are moments, not an attitude about life. My goal is to enjoy every minute and savor the short time that we have in every stage. As we have grown with Sydney, we have learned that part of that enjoyment is discovering that every little accomplishment is worth striving for. Our expectations have changed; we slow down and appreciate the gains that might be small for others, but are monumental for her. Her autism is not a huge disappointment anymore. It has made parenting all of our children more meaningful and more rewarding. We have found gratitude for the way her autism transforms all of us.

President Boyd K Packer said,

> "You parents and you families whose lives must be reordered because of a handicapped one, whose resources and time must be devoted to them, are special heroes. You are manifesting the works of God with every thought, with every gesture of tenderness and care you extend to the handicapped loved one. Never mind the tears nor the hours of regret and discouragement; never mind the times when you feel you cannot stand another day of what is required. You are living the principles of the gospel of Jesus Christ in exceptional purity. *And you perfect yourselves in the process.*
>
> Now, in all of this there must be balance, for the handicapped have responsibility to work out their own salvation. The nearer the normal patterns of conduct and discipline apply to the handicapped, the happier they will be.

Rebekah J. Shumway

> Every quarter of an inch of physical and mental improvement is worth striving for. The Prophet Joseph Smith said that "all the minds and spirits that God ever sent into the world are susceptible of enlargement." (*Teachings of the Prophet Joseph Smith*, p. 354).
>
> (Boyd K. Packer, "The Moving of the Water," *Ensign*, May 1991, 7)

Autism was a package from God that I did not want. I prayed and fought to send it back, but that was not what would have been best for us. Sydney's autism was a gift from a loving Heavenly Father, whose purpose and glory is our eternal life and salvation. There is nothing contrary to that glory in autism, in fact, the opposite is true. Sydney's autism made us "experts" in a field we previously knew nothing about. It made it a thrill anytime she will interact with her brothers. Not only are her advances exciting, autism taught us to slow down and appreciate the amazing growth of her brothers.

We entered a new world of people, and it brought friendships into our lives that we will cherish forever. It taught us to love others better; it taught us understanding for people who are different from us. It taught us patience and love for people who are socially awkward. It gave us appreciation for little accomplishments and the miracle and wonder of human intellect and interaction. Autism taught us about charity, the true love of Christ, loving unconditionally without expecting love in return. It humbled me, and brought me closer to the Savior who gave everything for us.

At the very beginning of our autism adventure, my dad told me that someday I would consider Sydney's autism a blessing, not a trial. I think in response to that I said something like, "I hope so," but I know I was thinking, "That sounds really romantic, but you do not have a grasp of what we are in for." Now I am starting to see his perspective. I would not go so far as to say I am grateful that Sydney has autism. If I could change her tomorrow, I would. In fact, I work every single day with her, trying to teach her to better communicate with us and to enjoy her life more. We went through a period when Spencer prayed almost daily, "Bless Sydney to lose her autism." I laughed at this prayer; it made it sound like autism was a sheet over her head that she might be able to shake off on a sharp turn! Deep inside, I hoped he was right.

We pray for changes every day. In spite of this, I know for certain that we have been blessed by Sydney's autism. It was not a curse given to our family, or a terrible tragedy. It has been a means for the Lord to lift us higher and teach us important lessons about life. It has made us all better people, and changed the way I parent and the way I perceive others and myself. Sydney's autism has been a gift. I think if I had my way, I would have returned it immediately upon opening it, but I know that it has been God's will, and that God's purposes are being accomplished through her autism. It has opened up a new world for us, and has strengthened and improved us as a family.

I would still give back the gift of autism if I could, but I wouldn't want to give back *all* of it. I know for certain that I wouldn't want to give back all the lessons, the friendships, the growth, and the precious memories that have come as a result of her autism.

One evening a few months after Sydney's fourth birthday I was bathing the kids and Spencer asked, "Mommy, now that Sydney is four, does she still have autism?" I answered, "Yes honey, she still has autism." He looked very disappointed. In a few moments he asked, "Will she have autism when she is ten?" My heart was breaking, "Yes, she will have autism when she is ten." I knew what was coming, and I knew what I had to tell him. "Will she have autism when she is twenty?" I sat back on my feet and sighed, "Sweetheart, Sydney will get better and better her whole life, but there are always going to be things that are harder for her than other people. She is going to have a little bit of autism her whole life." "Oh." came the reply. I was about to elaborate on the fact that Sydney is doing so well, and we are happy because she has learned how to talk... and Spencer cheerfully said, "But she won't have autism anymore when she resurrects!"

Sydney's autism is about this life. It is about living in this life, preparing for the next life. She will not have autism when she resurrects, and we will know her without the interference of her disability. Sydney is not thwarted eternally by her autism, and we should not define her by autism in this life. Her autism does not keep her from us; it is facilitating our perfection so we can have her forever.

Learning to see the gifts that come with autism has been comforting and gives us renewed strength to face each day. At the same time, Sydney's autism hasn't gone away. Although we see progress week-to-week or month-to-month, she still has autism disorder. As she matures new challenges will come, whether they are social, emotional, or physical. As a result of this, there is still pain and perhaps always will be. Though we have different expectations for Sydney, there will always be the yearning to know her more fully without the shadow of autism. There will still be days of frustration, fear and sadness. But through the mercy of a loving God we have been strengthened to see the blessings that can come through this challenge. They may not be the blessings we would have chosen, but they are the ones we need to be truly happy.

Like all trials in life, we can allow her autism to alienate us from God, or to refine us and change us to be more like the Savior. As we allow ourselves to be changed, we are one step closer to the kingdom of God. The scriptures tell us that there is no greater gift that we could receive.

> "If thou wilt do good, yea, and hold out faithful to the end, thou shalt be saved in the kingdom of God, which is the greatest of all the gifts of God; for there is no gift greater than the gift of salvation." (Doctrine and Covenants 6:13)

Sydney teaches us a lot about doing "good." Her autism is part of God's plan of happiness for our family. I have learned that happiness does not come in spite of her autism, but that her autism facilitates greater happiness for all of us: family, teachers and friends, who are lucky enough to love her.

It has been a joy to discover that autism is a gift.

Rebekah J. Shumway

ACKNOWLEDGEMENTS

There are not words to adequately thank the many people who have blessed our lives, nor is it possible to name them all, but here is the short list:

Our love and gratitude goes out to the staff, therapists and teachers at:

- Easter Seals in San Antonio;

- Franklin County Board of Mental Retardation and Developmental Disabilities, Early Childhood Education-Home Based Services;

- Ohio State University Speech-Language-Hearing Clinic;

- Upper Arlington City Schools, Intervention Services, *The Teddy Bear Class*;

- Jefferson County Public Schools;

- The enthusiastic and inventive nursery, primary and music teachers in the Church of Jesus Christ of Latter-day Saints;

- And finally; the Sawayas, Shumways and friends who surround our family with love and support. God has been very good to us.

THANK YOU!

Becky's Book Review List

Here is a review list that I have put together of books and websites that we have found useful. Most of it would be useful in helping children with any developmental disability.

Superflex...A Superhero Social Thinking Curriculum, Michelle Winner and Stephanie Madrigal

Playing, Laughing and Learning with Children on the Autism Spectrum, Julia Moor

Relationship Development Intervention with Young Children, Steven Gutstein
Also see www.rdiconnect.com.

The Child with Special Needs, Stanley Greenspan

The Affect-Based Language Curriculum (ABLC), Stanley Greenspan

The Out-of-Sync Child Has Fun, Carol Kranowitz

Siblings without Rivalry, Adele Faber

The BabyBumblebee Videos. www.babybumblebee.com

Signing Times Videos www.signingtime.com

www.playproject.org
This is the website for *The P.L.A.Y. Project* — which is the training set up by a Michigan pediatrician (Dr. Rick Solomon) to help parents do play-based ABA therapy at home.

www.difflearn.com
The Different Roads to Learning Store. I have spent a small fortune buying flashcards from these folks over the years. It is a great little online store.

www.iancommunity.org
This is a website community that has a ton of great information. See what others are doing to help their children with ASD.

Right From the Start, Sandra L. Harris and Mary Jane Gill-Weiss

Activities for Developing Pre-Skill Concepts, Toni Flowers

Russell is Extra Special, Charles A. Amenta

Parent Survival Manual; A Guide to Crisis Resolution in Autism and Related Developmental Disorders, Eric Schopler

Autism; Understanding the Disorder, Gary B. Mesibov, Lynn W. Adams and Laura G. Klinger

Children with Autism; a Parent's Guide, Michael D. Powers

The World of the Autistic Child, Bryna Siegel

Andy and His Yellow Frisbee, Mary Thompson

Ian's Walk, Laurie Lears

Activity Schedules for Children with Autism, Lynn E. McClannahan and Patricia J. Krantz

Handbook of Autism and Pervasive Developmental Disorders, Donald J. Cohen and Fred R. Volkmar

Teaching Language to Children with Autism or Other Developmental Disabilities, Mark L. Sundberg and James W. Partington

The Assessment of Basic Language and Learning Skills, (ABLSS), Mark L. Sundberg and James W. Partington

The Gift of Autism can be purchased at www.Lulu.com.